HAMAS, CAIR

and the

MUSLIM

BROTHERHOOD

HAMAS, CAIR, AND THE MUSLIM BROTHERHOOD

The Secret Plot to Destroy America

By Ilana Freedman

Center for Security Policy Press

For more information about this book, visit
SECUREFREEDOM.ORG

Hamas, Cair, and the Muslim Brotherhood
is published in the United States
by the Center for Security Policy Press,
a division of the Center for Security Policy.

ISBN-13: 978-1978249585
ISBN-10: 1978249586

The Center for Security Policy
Washington, D.C.
Phone: 202-835-9077
Email: info@SecureFreedom.org
For more information, visit SecureFreedom.org

Book design by Bravura Books

"The Ikhwan must understand that their work in America is a kind of grand Jihad in eliminating and destroying the Western civilization from within and "sabotaging" its miserable house by their hands and the hands of the believers so that it is eliminated and God's religion is made victorious over all other religions."

From the text of "An Explanatory Memorandum"

CONTENTS

INTRODUCTION

Hamas in the Middle East has been a practitioner of violent Islamic terrorism for three decades. Its ferocious jihad against Israel has been the cause of thousands of deaths on both sides. The presence of Hamas in the United States, however, has been less open and its mandate has undergone a transformation. Its presence here, and the threat it poses to America, have been debated, disputed, and denied for decades.

In the quest for truth, exposing the real and current threat that Hamas poses to America is difficult at best. Even establishing the very existence of Hamas in America is problematic, because in the United States, Hamas is a ghost organization, hiding behind well-guarded veils of secrecy, and protected by those considered 'respectable' representatives of the Muslim American community. The presence of Hamas in the U.S. is therefore generally overlooked by the average American, who would, no doubt, be astonished to know just how deeply the organization has infiltrated the institutions of America's political, societal, and government infrastructure.

Hamas' active presence in the United States is easy to miss, but it has been so well-documented that it is, by now, beyond question. Hamas is the Palestinian branch of the jihadist Muslim Brotherhood in Gaza and its presence in the U.S. is no less a threat here than is its counterpart in the Middle East. Only its methods are different; the threat that it poses is just as real.

Those who challenge the myth that Hamas does not exist in America are mocked and labeled as "Islamophobes" by both Muslim society and the politically correct. For the PC population, it is easier and more comfortable to reject both empirical evidence and judicial findings, and choose to believe that they are safe in a country where, they have convinced themselves, terrorism is only an occasional aberration and Islamic subversion doesn't exist.

As noted above, Hamas is the Palestinian branch of the Muslim Brotherhood (MB) based in Gaza, but operates in the West generally and the United States (U.S.) specifically under the secret cloak provided by a host of Brotherhood organizations. The most prominent of these is the Council on American-Islamic Relations (CAIR), which purports to be a community service organization, but in fact serves as the public face of the underground Hamas in America. With such support, and the fund-raising efforts of scores of what appear to be reputable companies and charitable organizations, Hamas in the Middle East in the past received millions of dollars in funding from its allies in the United States. The network of organizations from which the money flowed has been clearly defined and its intentions well-documented for decades. Although in the aftermath of the 2008 Holy Land Foundation Hamas terror funding trial, the financial *modus operandi* of the U.S. MB changed significantly, there is no question that in its early days, the U.S.-based Muslim Brotherhood (or Islamic Movement, as it calls itself), provided substantial funding back to its Middle East hub.

Hamas' primary goal, as described unequivocally in its Covenant (See Appendix I), is the violent destruction of Israel and the establishment of a global Islamic state ruled by Islamic Law (shariah). In May 2017, Hamas rolled out a new document with great fanfare (See Appendix II). Called, "A Document of General Principles and Policies," it was intended to convince the world that Hamas had become a somehow milder version of its former self.

In reality, although some cosmetic changes were made to the original Covenant that it purported to replace, it remains the same declaration of enmity to the Jewish State of Israel that it has always been. The new text substitutes the term 'Zionist enemy' in place of 'Jews', and says Hamas accepts the 1967 'borders,' but still does not recognize the Jewish State of Israel, a distinction which cancels out the concession on borders. Indeed, no Islamic entity could ever renounce jihad against either Jews in general or Israel in particular, because Islamic doctrine, law, and history all prohibit it.

The document also calls for "the full and complete liberation of Palestine, from the river to the sea" by means of armed "resistance." underscoring its continued determination to completely obliterate the state of Israel. Notably, too, this document rather belatedly and entirely unconvincingly tries to distance Hamas from its parent organization, the Muslim Brotherhood, the organization that created it and to which it is inextricably tied.

Hamas' role in the U.S. began in 1987, only months after it was founded in Gaza. Its original U.S. role was to raise funds to support its campaign of terrorism in the Middle East against Israel. Under the protection and guidance of the American branch of the Muslim Brotherhood, Hamas then expanded its operations in the U.S. to include the infiltration of American society, with the ultimate aim of turning the United States into an Islamic country, ruled under shariah (Islamic Law).

If this sounds far-fetched and hardly credible, Nihad Awad, co-founder and Executive Director of CAIR since its founding, publicly underscored the core principle when he read the key quote from the "Explanatory Memorandum on the General Strategic Goal for the Group in North America,"[1] at a 1994 symposium at Barry University in Florida:

> *"The Ikhwan [Muslim Brotherhood] must understand that their work in America is a kind of grand Jihad in eliminating and destroying the Western civilization from within and 'sabotaging' its miserable house by their hands and the hands of the believers*

---

[1] The Explanatory Memorandum on the General Strategic Goal for the Group in North America, written in 1991 by Mohamed Akram, a senior Muslim Brotherhood official, has served as a blueprint for Muslim Brotherhood's program in the United States (see Appendix II for full text).

so that it is eliminated and God's religion is made victorious over all other religions."[2]

One thing should be understood from the outset:
Hamas in the United States, as in Gaza, *is* the Muslim Brotherhood, and CAIR is its public face in America.

The degree of deception that the Brotherhood has employed to support Hamas' terrorist activities in the Middle East, while maintaining its secrecy in America, is perhaps stunning, but in accord with Muhammad's dictum that *'war is deceit'*, entirely to be expected. In today's world of political correctness run amok, the Muslim Brotherhood (*Ikhwan*) and its off-spring, Hamas and CAIR (among thousands of others), have eaten into the very fabric of American life with only one mission – to destroy it from within, as the Explanatory Memorandum plainly stated, and as Awad publicly reaffirmed.

In October 1997, the U.S. State Department designated Hamas a terrorist organization, in accordance with "section 219 of the Immigration and Nationality Act (INA), as amended."[3] But while the designation may have implications overseas, Hamas operatives remain free to function throughout the U.S., protected by a network of legitimate companies and not-for-profit organizations, and behind the shield provided by its American face and voice, CAIR.

With significant initial support from the international Muslim Brotherhood at a minimum, Hamas has become a part of a large and complex nationwide system with two guiding principles: the destruction of Israel (and Jewish people everywhere) as proclaimed in its Covenent, and the Islamification of America.

The subject at hand is complex, and there is an extraordinary amount of documentary evidence to support the assertions in this monograph. This volume, therefore, only scratches the surface.

Nevertheless, the monograph will refute the argument that Hamas does not exist in America, and will explore the many ways in which Hamas has abused the freedoms that America provides in order to accomplish its goals. By exploiting our open society, easy access to resources, and an environment of rampant denial and political correctness, Hamas has been able to build strong positions from which to wage its own two-pronged

---

[2] The Explanatory Memorandum, seized by the FBI in a 2004 raid and presented by the Department of Justice in the 2008 Holy Land Foundation trial, was published as a monograph by the Center for Security Policy in 2016. http://www.centerforsecuritypolicy.org/wp-content/uploads/2014/05/Explanatory_Memoradum.pdf

[3] Foreign Terrorist Organizations. Bureau of Counterterrorism, US State Department. http://www.state.gov/j/ct/rls/other/des/123085.htm

program: violent jihad against Israel and the Jews, and civilization jihad against America.

This volume will disclose Hamas' overlapping and interconnected alliances to its parent organization, the Muslim Brotherhood; its shield, CAIR; and the host of other closely-linked organizations that support it. It will show how the unholy liaison among Hamas, CAIR, and the Muslim Brotherhood has become a nexus through which an agenda to destroy both Israel by force and America by subversion has been developed.[4]

Finally, it will reveal how the Hamas/CAIR/Muslim Brotherhood nexus poses a threat, not just to Israel, but to the fundamental principles on which the United States was founded, and thus to America itself.

---

[4] References to Israel throughout the monograph are an essential part of the story, since Hamas' obsession with the destruction of Israel is central to its core mission, both in the Middle East and in America.

PART I

Hamas Discovers America

From its founding in 1987, Hamas in Gaza needed to raise funds to support its terror campaign against Israel. It first turned to established Islamic bankers like the al-Taqwa Bank, and sympathetic regimes like Iran. But early on, Hamas leaders saw the need for a more consistent source of funding to support its program of war against Israel. For this, Hamas turned to the West.

Putting On a New Face

When Hamas began to operate in the United States in 1987, its leaders realized it needed a new persona. A program of terrorism in the United States would be clearly counter-productive at that phase of the agenda, because it would prevent Hamas from achieving its goal to fund its operations in the Middle East. Its leaders therefore developed a program of economic activity for its new, 'friendly' face in the West, one that would support these objectives without calling attention to the deadly violence it was underwriting. At the same time, it needed to operate under a veil of secrecy, because despite its pretense, it was well-known as an anti-Israel, antisemitic, terrorist organization. Moreover, because Hamas operated under the wing of the Muslim Brotherhood, its founder and patron, its goals expanded to include not only funding its jihad against Israel, now cloaked in secrecy, but also the Brotherhood's Civilization Jihad in America.

The Brotherhood's ultimate goals were stated openly by Islamic activist Abdurahman Alamoudi, who told the 1996 annual convention of the Islamic Association of Palestine in Illinois, *"It depends on me and you, either we do it now or we do it after a hundred years, but this country will become a Muslim country. And I [think] if we are outside this country we can say oh, Allah, destroy America, but once we are here, our mission in this country is to change it."*[5]

'An Explanatory Memorandum'

The story of Hamas in America is closely connected to both its history in Gaza and its strong affiliation with the Muslim Brotherhood. It began in 1987, the same year Hamas was founded in Gaza, with the initial drafting of

---

[5] "Abdulrahman Alamoudi - Head of American Muslim Council goes to jail for 23 years" October 29, 2004. MilitantIslamMonitor.org
http://www.militantislammonitor.org/article/id/306

a secret document for the Brotherhood, called "An Explanatory Memorandum." (See Appendix III for the full text).

The document, which was not distributed internally until 1991, was entitled "An Explanatory Memorandum: On the General Strategic Goal for the Group in North America." The 'Memorandum' was authored and signed by Mohamed Akram.

Akram, whose full name is Mohamed Akram Adlouni, has been variously listed as a Muslim Brotherhood operative,[6] a secretary in the Muslim Brotherhood,[7] and a member of the Board of Directors for the Muslim Brotherhood in North America, and senior Hamas leader.[8] He is also the General Secretary of the Lebanese Al Quds International Foundation[9], which received the special designation of Global Terrorist entity in 2012.[10] The designation, which was pursuant to Executive Order 13224 of 2001,[11] denied financial and material support to terrorists and their facilitators. The Al Quds Foundation was cited for both being controlled by, and for acting on behalf of, Hamas.[12]

In 1987, the Treasury Department commented on the designation:

"Hamas's leadership runs all of the foundation's affairs through Hamas members who serve on the Board of Trustees, the Board of Directors, and other administrative committees. All documents, plans, budgets, and projects of Al-Quds are drafted by Hamas officials. Several senior Hamas officials, including Specially Designated Global Terrorists Musa Abu-Marzuq and Usama Hamdan, served on Al-Quds' Board of Trustees. Representatives at

---

[6] "The Muslim Brotherhood's "General Strategic Goal" For North America" by DiscovertheNetworks.org
http://www.discoverthenetworks.org/viewSubCategory.asp?id=1235

[7] "Pamela Geller And The Anti-Islam Movement" by David Shipler. The New Yorker, May 12, 2015. http://www.newyorker.com/news/news-desk/pamela-geller-and-the-anti-islam-movement

[8] Muslim Brotherhood in America, by the Center for Security Policy, 2013.
http://www.centerforsecuritypolicy.org/wp-content/uploads/2014/05/Explanatory_Memoradum.pdf

[9] Al-Quds International Forum Website http://www.alquds-forum.com/en/index.php?s=contact

[10] "Treasury Sanctions Two Hamas-Controlled Charities: Actions Target Lebanon-based Al-Waqfiya and Al-Quds Charities" U.S. Department of the Treasury, October 4, 2012.
https://www.treasury.gov/press-center/press-releases/Pages/tg1725.aspx

[11] "Executive Order 13224" Department of State. September 23, 2001
https://www.state.gov/j/ct/rls/other/des/122570.htm

[12] "Treasury Sanctions Two Hamas-Controlled Charities - Actions Target Lebanon-based Al-Waqfiya and Al-Quds Charities" U.S. Department of the Treasury Press Center, October 4, 2012.
https://www.treasury.gov/press-center/press-releases/Pages/tg1725.aspx

*an Al-Quds conference were told to consider themselves unofficial
ambassadors for Hamas in their respective countries."* [13]

"An Explanatory Memorandum" can best be described as a proposal for a secret long-range strategic plan to transform the United States into an Islamic country governed under Islamic law (shariah). It would later be adopted by the Muslim Brotherhood for its program in the United States.[14] The plan describes the recommended strategies and tactics to be promoted and implemented by the Muslim Brotherhood, including the of building of a network of interconnected organizations that formed the funding and program facilitation chains. Akram concluded the document with a list of 29 like-minded organizations in America, about which he wrote:

*"A list of our organizations and the organizations of our friends.
[Imagine if they all march according to one plan!!!]"* [15]

These were groups that had been founded by the Muslim Brotherhood to further its strategic plan, many of which were later placed on the list of "unindicted co-conspirators" by the U.S. Department of Justice at the 2008 conclusion of the Holy Land Foundation Hamas terror funding trial in Dallas, TX.

The "Memorandum" was based on ideas that were put forward in 1987, but wasn't approved or distributed by the Ikhwan until 1991. Even after it was distributed to its circle of followers, the document remained secret for another eleven years, while the Brotherhood built out its network of organizations. The document might have remained hidden for much longer, but for the discovery that the Holy Land Foundation in Richardson, Texas, was the lead agency in an active money laundering operation for Hamas. The trail led to other organizations and in the spring of 2002, landed the investigation in northern Virginia.

On March 21, 2002, U. S. Treasury Department released a statement that Federal agents had raided fifteen organizations and individuals in Herndon, Virginia, a quiet residential community, about 20 miles from Washington, DC. A search warrant was also issued for the Mar-Jac halal chicken farm in Georgia. The homes and offices listed in the search included companies and officers associated with the Safa Group, suspected of laundering money for Hamas and other terrorist organizations.

The Safa Group was an umbrella organization for over a hundred companies and not-for-profits, which served as a network for supporting several terrorist organizations, most particularly Hamas. While the Holy

---

[13] Ibid.

[14] "The Muslim Brotherhood's "General Strategic Goal" For North America" Discover the Networks http://www.discoverthenetworks.org/viewSubCategory.asp?id=1235

[15] See the list of organizations at the end of the full text of the "Memorandum" in Appendix II.

Land Foundation was not part of the Safa Group, it was used as a conduit through which members of the Safa Group and other Brotherhood-connected organizations could raise and launder millions of dollars for the benefit of Hamas operations against Israel.

According to journalist Judith Miller[16], one of the primary targets of the massive search was the complex of buildings at 555 Grove Street and 550 Grove Street in Herndon, Va., where a host of Islamic organizations, including the Saudi-funded charity, the SAAR Foundation, had offices. Miller reported that "more than 150 agents and officers of the Customs Service, the Internal Revenue Service and several other Treasury agencies" participated in the search, along with local Virginia police. Although no arrests were made that day, agents questioned a number of employees and residents, and carried away many loads of documents and computers.

Muslim organizations cried foul. The Washington Report on Middle Eastern Affairs, an openly pro-Palestinian, anti-Israel publication, decried "the assault on American Muslims' civil liberties and the selective targeting of their institutions, organizations and charities," and blamed the raids on "hate-mongers, Islamophobes, and others with special agendas." It reported that among the sites raided were the International Institute of Islamic Thought (IIIT), the Graduate School of Islamic and Social Sciences, the Fiqh Council of North America, and the Virginia office of the Muslim World League. At a press conference sponsored by CAIR, prominent Muslim organizations and leaders immediately denounced the raids as a "fishing expedition" and "McCarthy-like witch hunt."[17]

But despite the outcry from Muslim organizations and media, the raid netted a large haul of incriminating intelligence about the strategies and tactics of the groups and their secret support for Hamas.

Then, in August 2004, two off-duty Baltimore County police officers saw Ismail Selim Elbarasse driving over Maryland's Chesapeake Bay Bridge, while his wife, whose head was covered by a hijab, videotaped the bridge from their SUV. He claimed she was only photographing boats in the bay, but her videotape was subsequently found to include tight shots of the bridge's cables, "the bridge joints of the main support system," and other structural components that were "integral to the structural integrity of the bridge."[18] According to the police report, "A check through NCIC revealed, Ismael Selim Elbarasse was a person of interest from the FBI as having

---

[16] "A NATION CHALLENGED: THE MONEY TRAIL; Raids Seek Evidence of Money-Laundering", by Judith Miller. New york Times, March 21, 2002
http://www.nytimes.com/2002/03/21/us/a-nation-challenged-the-money-trail-raids-seek-evidence-of-money-laundering.html

[17] Ibid.

[18] Search Warrant for 4502 Whistler Court, Annandale, Virginia. August 31, 2004. United States District Court, Eastern Distric of Virginia,

possible ties with terrorism."[19] Elbarasse was arrested and held as a material witness for two weeks, after which he was released under house arrest.

The Discovery of 'An Explanatory Memorandum'

On Saturday, 21 August 2004, federal agents executed a search warrant on Elbarasse's home, garage, and car.

Piled throughout the home and garage, agents found what proved to be the archives of the Muslim Brotherhood in North America. From the Center for Security Policy's account of the discovery, we learn that '[a]mong the 80 banker-boxes worth of documents discovered there were papers that confirmed what investigators and counterterrorism experts had long suspected and contended about the myriad Muslim-American groups in the United States: nearly all of them are controlled by the Muslim Brotherhood."[20] The huge haul of these archives contained detailed information about a long list of Hamas-linked organizations in America, associated with and controlled by the Muslim Brotherhood.

Among the documents they found, was a single copy of the "Explanatory Memorandum," a small but significant discovery. Another important find was a 1992 memo, entitled "Islamic Action for Palestine - An internal memo." The memo described the history of the Muslim Brotherhood's program and its network in the U.S. It also described its relationship with Hamas in Gaza, which it called its "tool and striking wing." (See a full translation in Appendix IV)

The memo gave details about the decisions reached by the Brotherhood to "[support] the continuation of the intifada" in Israel, and "the completion of formation of Palestine committees... publicizing and focusing on the savagery of the Jews in Palestine."[21] Its overriding message was justified by one of its two defining "characteristics":

> *... the struggle is with the Jews who do not constitute a danger to Palestine alone, but a danger to Arabs and Muslims in their homelands, resources, religion, traditions, influence and political entity. Due to the Jewish influence in different global nations specially America and Europe, the struggle in Palestine has a degree of entanglement and complexity, or junctions and*

---

[19] Maryland Transportation Department Police Department, August 20, 2004. https://www.investigativeproject.org/documents/case_docs/1523.pdf

[20] "From the Archives of the Muslim Brotherhood - An Explanatory Memorandum." Center for Security Policy, 2013. https://www.centerforsecuritypolicy.org/wp-content/uploads/2014/05/Explanatory_Memoradum.pdf

[21] "Backgrounder: The Holy Land Foundation for Relief and Development." Anti-Defamation League archives. http://archive.adl.org/nr/exeres/83323767-981c-4e4d-9b77-70dd604d2d75,db7611a2-02cd-43af-8147-649e26813571,frameless.html

contradictions between international politics like no other cause in the world."[22]

Agents also found a 1992 letter from the Islamic Relief Committee[23], requesting weapons and financial support, and extolling the killing of Jews:

"You do not know how happy people become when they watch those Mujahideen and how proud they feel when they parade in their uniforms and weapons and the extent of their honor when they carry out their Jihadist operations against the Jews and their tentacles.... Jihad in Palestine is different from any Jihad; the meaning of killing a Jew for the liberation of Palestine cannot be compared to any Jihad on earth...provide us with what helps us of funds and weapons. Weapons, weapons, our brothers."[24]

According to court records, agents also seized a large collection of computer disks, bank records and Arabic language documents, including one document enttitled "For Your Eyes Only -- How to Propagate Islam, " as well as copies of checks from the Dar Al-Hijra mosque in Falls Church; a piece of paper containing the address of the Norfolk Naval Station; Israeli travel documents; various "anti-Israel materials"; and documents concerning the Muslim Brotherhood.[25]

Ismail Elbarasse was hardly an innocent bystander. He was formerly a board member of the Islamic Association for Palestine (IAP), and an assistant to Mousa Abu Marzook, who was a senior Hamas operative in the U.S. at the time, and with whom Elbarasse once shared a bank account. He was also a member of the Palestine Committee (PALCOM), one of the first organizations founded by the Brotherhood to support Hamas in the U.S. PALCOM's by-laws made its mission and its connection to the Brotherhood crystal clear:

"Palestine Committee is a specialized committee emanating from the Palestine Section which was formed by the executive office of the Muslim Brotherhood in the Levant countries. Its scope of work

---

[22] Islamic Action for Palestine -*An* internal memo - October - 1992

[23] The Islamic Relief Committee was a not-for-profit recipient of Holy Land Foundation funding.

[24] Backgrounder: The Holy Land Foundation for Relief and Development
http://archive.adl.org/nr/exeres/83323767-981c-4e4d-9b77-70dd604d2d75,db7611a2-02cd-43af-8147-649e26813571,frameless.html

[25] "Va. Man Tied to Hamas Held as Witness" *by Eric Rich and Jerry Markon.* Washington Post, August 25, 2004http://www.washingtonpost.com/wp-dyn/articles/A28476-2004Aug24.html

is limited to North America and its contacts include other countries."[26]

The Dar al-Hijrah mosque in nearby Falls Church, Virginia, of which Elbarasse was a co-founder, is a well- known hotbed of Islamic jihad, where American-born Islamic cleric Anwar al-Awlaki served as Imam. In 2002, Awlaki left the U.S for Yemen, where he played a leading role in al-Qaeda of the Arabian Peninsula (AQAP).[27] Prior to his departure and long after his death, al-Awlaki inspired an entire generation of jihadis,[28] including Major Nidal Hasan, who murdered thirteen people in a shooting spree at Fort Hood, Texas, in 2009; the Tsarnaev brothers, who set off two pressure-cooker bombs at the Boston Marathon in 2013; and the Kouachi brothers, who carried out the Charlie Hebdo attack in Paris in 2015.

The discoveries in Elbarasse's home shone a spotlight on the true mission of the Muslim Brotherhood in America: the creation of the complex web of inter-linked companies and organizations, whose goal was to assist in the civilization jihad of the Muslim Brotherhood and support of Hamas in Gaza. Significant among these were the intricate connections among the Muslim Brotherhood, CAIR, and Hamas. They firmly established the Brotherhood's paramount mission in America as outlined in the Memorandum.

Making America an Islamic State

Although the Muslim Brotherhood went to great lengths to hide its numerous activities and even its presence in the U.S., the message of the Memorandum was unambivalent. The document was explicit in acknowledging that "the Ikhwan" was single-minded in its mission to carry out its "work in America."

The Memorandum was drafted, according to Akram, to present Islam "as a civilization alternative," and to "support the global Islamic State wherever it is."[29] Under the heading "Understanding the role of the Muslim Brother in North America," Akram is at his most explicit:

---

[26] "Bylaws of the Palestine Committee of the Muslim Brotherhood" Investigation Project. http://www.investigativeproject.org/document/24-bylaws-of-the-palestine-committee-of-the-muslim

[27] Al-Awlaki was killed in a U.S. drone strike in Yemen in September 2011

[28] "The American who inspires terror from Paris to the U.S." By Peter Bergen. CNN, January 12, 2015. http://www.cnn.com/2015/01/11/opinion/bergen-american-terrorism-leader-paris-attack/

[29] Note that in 1987, the "Islamic State" was a conceptual construct relating to the global caliphate as a goal to be obtained, rather than the terrorist group we know today, currently wreaking havoc around the world under the banner of the "Islamic State."

"The process of settlement is a "Civilization-Jihadist Process" with all the word means. The Ikhwan must understand that their work in America is a kind of grand Jihad in eliminating and destroying the Western civilization from within and "sabotaging" its miserable house by their hands and the hands of the believers so that it is eliminated and God's religion is made victorious over all other religions. Without this level of understanding, we are not up to this challenge and have not prepared ourselves for Jihad yet. It is a Muslim's destiny to perform Jihad and work wherever he is and wherever he lands until the final hour comes, and there is no escape from that destiny except for those who chose to slack."

In an effort to implement its ambitious plans, the Muslim Brotherhood has been methodical and highly effective. The question of whether the Memorandum was an imperative or merely a proposal has been argued since its discovery, but the point is irrelevant. Regardless of whether or not it was officially adopted as a guiding document, the suggestions it contains have been followed closely by the Brotherhood as it has built out its program in

Anwar al-Awlaki in AQAP photo posing with a shoulder-mounted missile launcher (MANPAD)
(Photo: SITE Intelligence Group, via Agence France-Presse)

the U.S. Using the methodology outlined in the Memorandum as a starting point, the Brotherhood established a dense network of interconnected organizations that have served as fronts for both laundering money for Hamas and infiltrating American life at every level. Camouflaged as legitimate companies, charitable organizations, and financial institutions, the network provides cover for the overarching Brotherhood network. The organizations support each other within the network to fulfill the Brotherhood goals, and when one company or charitable foundation is forced to close, it is simply replaced by another with a new name to carry on its work.

Another document found in Elbarasse's Virginia home is an undated and unsourced paper which described how the Brotherhood plan to Islamize America would play out. Called "Phases of the World Underground

Movement Plan," it lists the five phases that the Muslim Brotherhood Movement in North America would go through to achieve its goals.[30]

"Phase One: Phase of discreet and secret establishment of leadership.

"Phase Two: Phase of gradual appearance on the public scene and exercising and utilizing various public activities (It greatly succeeded in implementing this stage). It also succeeded in achieving a great deal of its important goals, such as infiltrating various sectors of the Government. Gaining religious institutions and embracing senior scholars. Gaining public support and sympathy. Establishing a shadow government (secret) within the Government.

"Phase Three: Escalation phase, prior to conflict and confrontation with the rulers, through utilizing mass media. Currently in progress.

"Phase Four: Open public confrontation with the Government through exercising the political pressure approach. It is aggressively implementing the above-mentioned approach. Training on the use of weapons domestically and overseas in anticipation of zero-hour. It has noticeable activities in this regard.

"Phase Five: Seizing power to establish their Islamic Nation under which all parties and Islamic groups are united."

The insight that this document gives into the "mindset, planning, and vision of the Islamic movement in North America"[31] is stunning. Although it is only known that the document was written prior to 2004, a look forward through the intervening thirteen years shows an alarming indication of how much of the plan has already been accomplished or is now in process.

By hiding its activities behind a long list of seemingly independent and unrelated organizations, the Muslim Brotherhood has emulated a tactic used by the Communist Party in the 1950s during the Cold War. The Communists created webs of interconnecting front groups in the United States to channel its movements, cover its infiltration activities, and confuse America's law enforcement by making its operations more difficult to identify and combat.[32]

---

[30] *Shariah: The Threat To America: An Exercise In Competitive Analysis* by William J. Boykin, Harry Edward Soyster, and Henry Cooper. As summarized in "The Muslim Brotherhood's Strategic Plan" http://shariahthethreat.org/a-short-course-1-what-is-shariahh/a-short-course-14-the-muslim-brotherhood's-strategic-plan/

[31] Ibid

[32] "Yuri Bezmenov: Deception was My Job" YouTube Video: Soviet Subversion of the Free-World Press (1984) Video interview by G. Edward Griffin's with Yuri Alexandrovich Bezmenov, former KGB agent, whose specialty was disinformation of Westerners visiting the Soviet Union.

Individual Muslim groups in America have provided similar channels to support Hamas. For example, according to the FBI, the Muslim student organization MAYA (Muslim American Youth Association) has "played pivotal roles in building Hamas's infrastructure in the United States . . . . MAYA served as a conduit for money to Hamas ... and served as a forum where Hamas could promote its ideology and recruit new members."[33]

MAYA conferences are well known for their inflammatory speakers, who have encouraged violent jihad and raised a great deal of money for Hamas. In December 1989, MAYA co-sponsored a Kansas City, Missouri conference with the Holy Land Foundation and IAP. The organization invited a speaker, whose face was hidden behind a veil to protect his identity. He proudly claimed that he had killed 16 Israelis in a bus attack, and the audience responded to his speech with cries of *Allahu Akbar!"* ("Allah is great!").[34]

At a subsequent MAYA convention, that took place between December 30, 1994, and January 2, 1995, in Los Angeles, Sheikh Muhammad Siyam, was the keynote speaker.[35] He was introduced as "Head of operations of Al Jihad Al Islamia in Gaza, the Hamas military wing."[36] In a blistering speech, Siyam said to the audience:

> *"I've been told to restrict or restrain what I say...I hope no one is recording me or taking any pictures, as none are allowed ... because I'm going to speak the truth to you. It's simple. Finish off the Israelis. Kill them all! Exterminate them! No peace ever! Do not bother to talk politics."* [37]

Siyam was introduced as "Head of operations of al-Jihad al-Islamia in Gaza, the HAMAS military wing." The FBI reported that $207,000 was raised

---

Bezmenov later escaped to the West in 1970. In this video, Bezmenov explains how the KGB utilized various individuals to undermine the Western society in its morals and values. https://www.youtube.com/watch?v=y3qkf3bajd4

[33] "Hate Preachers Fundraise For The Islamic Society Of Boston" by Sam Westrop. Americans for Peace and Tolerance. http://www.peaceandtolerance.org/2016/05/30/hate-preachers-fundraise-for-the-islamic-society-of-boston

[34] Ibid

[35] "Hate Preachers Fundraise For The Islamic Society Of Boston" May 30, 2016. http://www.peaceandtolerance.org/2016/05/30/hate-preachers-fundraise-for-the-islamic-society-of-boston/

[36] "The Homeland Security Implications of Radicalization" Testimony of Steven Emerson Before the United States House Committee on Homeland Security, Subcommittee on Intelligence, Information Sharing, and Terrorism Risk Assessment. September 20, 2006. http://www.investigativeproject.org/documents/testimony/20.pdf

[37] Ibid

from conference attendees for the benefit of the Holy Land Foundation,[38] which was subsequently convicted of funneling millions of dollars to Hamas.

While MAYA served a double purpose for the Hamas/CAIR/Muslim Brotherhood network (as fundraiser for Hamas and recruiter of hard-core activists for its American program), the Brotherhood also developed its program in other ways. One was a complex, covert program of infiltrating government at the local, state, and federal levels, running for and being elected to public office, and aggressively promoting the concepts of "pluralism," "multi-culturalism," and "diversity" in order to create an atmosphere in which any criticism of Islam in general or any Muslim in particular becomes a crime of "Islamophobia."

---

[38] "MIDEAST FLARE-UP: THE MONEY TRAIL; F.B.I. Traces Hamas's Plan To Finance Attacks to '93" by David Firestone. New York Times, December 6, 2001.
http://www.nytimes.com/2001/12/06/world/mideast-flare-up-money-trail-fbi-traces-hamas-s-plan-finance-attacks-93.htm

IAP – The Predecessor of CAIR

In 1981, Muslim Brotherhood leader and future Hamas secretary general Khalid Mashaal ordered the establishment of the Islamic Association for Palestine (IAP).[39] His order was carried out by Mousa Abu Marzook[40], and Ghassan Elashi's brother-in-law.

The IAP called itself "a not-for-profit, public-awareness, educational, political, social, and civic, national grassroots organization dedicated to advancing a just, comprehensive, and eternal solution to the cause of Palestine and suffrages [sic] of the Palestinians." It operated as a propaganda voice for Hamas, publishing pro-Hamas articles and organizing rallies.[41]

The government later described it as "the 'propaganda and information' organization that received money from Hamas leader Mousa Abu Marzook to provide Hamas propaganda in the United States."[42] A former chief of the FBI's counterterrorism department went even further, calling it "a front organization for Hamas that engage[d] in propaganda for Islamic militants."[43] In "An Explanatory Memorandum on the General Strategic Goal for the Group in North America," IAP was listed among the organizations affiliated with the Muslim Brotherhood in the United States.

In the late 1980s, Marzook participated in the founding of the Occupied Land Fund, which later changed its name to the Holy Land Foundation for Relief and Development (HLF). The reorganization that led to the name change enabled the Palestine Committee to comply with the Muslim Brotherhood's orders to "increase the financial and the moral support for Hamas," to "fight surrendering solutions" (like the Oslo Peace Accord[44]), and to publicize "the savagery of the Jews."[45] The new 'charity'

---

[39] "Council on American Islamic Relations (CAIR)"
http://brotherhoodunmasked.net/organizations-connected-to-the-muslim-brotherhood/cair

[40] Marzook became chairman of IAP's advisory committee and, over the years, has risen steadily in the ranks of Hamas. He now serves as Hamas's deputy political bureau chief in Cairo, Egypt.

[41] "Investigation Exposes AMP Leaders' Ties to Former U.S-Based Hamas-Support Network

IPT News, June 24, 2015. http://www.investigativeproject.org/4891/investigation-exposes-amp-leaders-ties-to-former

[42] *C.A.I.R. Is Hamas: How the Federal Government Proved that the Council on American Islamic Relations is a Front for Terrorism,* December 2, 2016.
http://www.centerforsecuritypolicy.org/2016/12/02/c-a-i-r-is-hamas/

[43] http://www.discoverthenetworks.org/individualProfile.asp?indid=676

[44] The Oslo Peace Accord (officially known as the Declaration of Principles) on Interim Self-Government Arrangements or short Declaration of Principles, signed by Palestinian leader Yassir Arafat and Israeli Prime Minister Yitzhak Rabin in 1993 and 1995, created the Palestinian Authority as a provisional government, and included a five-year schedule for

organization qualified as a 'not-for-profit', to which Marzook gave $210,000 in start-up capital.

An internal IAP memo dated October 1992 (see Appendix IV) revealed how its leadership laid down the principles of the organizations, its structure, and its mission. It made crystal clear that its primary mission was to destroy the Jews, not only in Israel, but throughout the world, including in America:

> *"Like other Western, Arab and Islamic arenas, the American arena has seen a move for action for the Palestinian cause .... The first organizational frame for Islamic action for Palestine came in the beginning of the eighties when the leadership of the Movement decided to establish "The Islamic Association for Palestine in North America." The Association was and still is the general field through which the Movement [Hamas] expresses its view and positions regarding the Palestinian cause."*

> *"Palestine is the one for which Muslim Brotherhood prepared armies - made up from the children of Islam in the Arab and Islamic nations - to liberate its land from the abomination and the defilement of the children of the Jews and they watered its pure soil with their honorable blood which sprouted into a Jihad that is continuing until the Day of Resurrection and provided a zeal without relenting*

The extent of the relationship and shared activities between IAP and HLF became even clearer when, in February 1996, an IAP activist told the FBI that IAP had routed $3 million of its fundraising proceeds annually to the Holy Land Foundation in Palestine, which rerouted it to Hamas.[46]

---

resolving all areas of conflict between the Palestinians and the Israelis. The Accords marked the first time that the Israel and the Palestine Liberation Organization (PLO) formally recognized each other.

[45] http://www.nationalreview.com/article/375620/roots-cairs-intimidation-campaign-andrew-c-mccarthy

[46] Memorandum to R. Richard Newcomb, Director of the Office for Foreign Assets Control, U.S. Department of the Treasury, by Dale L. Watson, Assistant Director for Counterterrorism, FBI.

The 'Philadelphia Conference'

Less than a month after the September 13, 1993, signing of the Oslo Peace Accord on the White House lawn, a secret summit of twenty-four leading Hamas members and supporters in the U.S. was held at a Courtyard by Marriott hotel in Philadelphia, Pennsylvania.[47] The meeting was billed as the "Future of Islamic Action for Palestine in North America Seminar, 2-3 October 1993." Its purpose was to plan how to move the Hamas strategy forward in the United States and undermine the Oslo peace accords. Oslo represented a step closer to a peace agreement between Israel and the Palestinians, an accommodation to which Hamas declared it would never agree.

Attending the meeting were senior leaders of the Muslim Brotherhood, the Holy Land Foundation, and the IAP. These included:

Musa Abu Marzook, head of Hamas' Political Bureau, who represented Hamas in the U.S. Known for his fundraising talent, he reached out to his connections with Muslim donors in the U.S. and is credited with helping it to further its military ambitions against Israel. In 1995, Marzook was listed by the US. Treasury Department as a Specially Designated Terrorist. In 2002, a U.S.

Musa Abu Marzook (Photo: Forward.com)

Federal Court indicted him for conspiring to violate U.S. laws against dealings in terrorist funds.[48]

Nihad Awad, who acted as IAP's Director of Public Relations and became the Executive Director of CAIR, upon its founding a year after the Philadelphia meeting. (He later said he couldn't remember attending the meeting.).[49]

---

[47] "The Roots of CAIR's Intimidation Campaign" by Andrew McCarthy. National Review, April 12, 2014 http://www.nationalreview.com/article/375620/roots-cairs-intimidation-campaign-andrew-c-mccarthy

[48] "Senior Leader Of Hamas and Texas Computer Company Indicted for Conspiracy to Violate U.S. Ban On Financial Dealings With Terrorists." Department of Justice Press Release, December 18, 2002.
https://www.justice.gov/archive/opa/pr/2002/December/02_crm_734.htm

[49] In October 2003, when asked if he attended the conference, he said "I don't remember." http://www.investigativeproject.org/redirect/Awad_I_Dont_Remember.pdf

Omar Ahmad,[50] (President of IAP, and a co-founder of CAIR). He later claimed he "did not recall attending the meeting, but FBI reported that he not only attended, he planned and moderated it.[51]

Others in attendance included men whom the FBI identified as "senior leaders of Hamas and money couriers in the West Bank and Gaza, the HLF, and the IAP."[52] They included:

Shukri Abu Baker, a co-founder of the HLF, who served as its President, Secretary, and Chief Executive Officer.

Haitham Maghawri, the foundation's Executive Director, who later faced trial in Texas for providing material support to Hamas.

Ghassan Elashi (who later denied he had been there).[53] He co-founded HLF[54] and served as its Treasurer and Chairman of the Board.[55] He also incorporated IAP and was a founding board member of CAIR's Texas chapter.

- Mohammad Al-Hanooti, former head of IAP, who, according to the FBI, "collected over six million U.S. dollars for support of HAMAS in Israel."[56]

- Ismail Elbarasse, who incorporated the American Middle Eastern League for Palestine, which "did business as" IAP.[57] In the 1990s, Elbarasse held a joint bank account with Mousa Abu Marzook and

---

[50] In 1998, journalist Lisa Gardiner quoted a speech he gave in California, "Islam isn't in America to be equal to any other faith, but to become dominant....The Koran, the Muslim book of scripture, should be the highest authority in America, and Islam the only accepted religion on Earth." He has denied saying it. "Did CAIR founder say Islam to rule America?" by Art Moore. *WorldNetDaily*, December 11, 2006. http://www.wnd.com/2006/12/39229/

[51] "Omar Ahmad and the Palestine Committee" https://www.investigativeproject.org/documents/misc/635.pdf

[52] *Hamas: Politics, Charity, and Terrorism in the Service of Jihad*. By Matthew Levitt. (2006). New Haven and London: Yale University Press. Chapter 6

[53] "MIDEAST FLARE-UP: THE MONEY TRAIL; F.B.I. Traces Hamas's Plan To Finance Attacks to '93" by David Firestone. *New York Times,* December 6, 2001. http://www.nytimes.com/2001/12/06/world/mideast-flare-up-money-trail-fbi-traces-hamas-s-plan-finance-attacks-93.html

[54] U.S. v. Holy Land Foundation (N.D. TX.), No. 3:04-CR-240-G, Government Exhibit 011-0032, http://www.nefafoundation.org/miscellaneous/HLF/AOI_OLF.pdf.

[55] U.S. v. Holy Land Foundation (N.D. TX.), No. 3:04-CR-240-G, Indictment, Filed July 26, 2004 http://www.anti-cair-net.org/93Phillyfinal.pdf

[56] "The 1993 Philadelphia Meeting: A Roadmap for Future Muslim Brotherhood Actions in the U.S." by NEFA Senior Analyst Josh Lefkowitz. NEFA Foundation, November 15, 2007. Reference: FBI Action Memorandum dated Nov. 5, 2001. http://www.anti-cair-net.org/93Phillyfinal.pdf

[57] U.S. v. Holy Land Foundation (N.D. TX.), No. 3:04-CR-240-G, Government Exhibit 011-0012. http://www.nefafoundation.org/miscellaneous/HLF/DBA_AMELP_TX.pdf.

was responsible for channeling the money raised to fund Hamas' military actions against Israel.

The FBI transcripts from its secret wiretaps of the Philadelphia meeting were later entered into evidence at the 2007-8 Holy Land Foundation (HLF) trial and showed a commitment on the part of the attendees to use the freedoms available to them in America to create a "safe place for the Movement."

Throughout the meeting, participants used coded references in their discussion of how best to support Hamas and avoid detection. The FBI wiretaps revealed that, for example, throughout the two days, the word "Samah" (Hamas backwards) was used instead of "Hamas." They discussed the "Union," a code name referring to the IAP, for which Awad was then spokesman. Awad himself was referred to simply as "Nihad."[58]

Over the course of the two days, it became clear that this was a congregation of Islamic movers and shakers in the U.S., coming together "to develop a strategy to defeat the Israeli/Palestinian peace accord, and to continue and improve their fund-raising and political activities in the United States."[59] Among the topics discussed were "how to redefine the perception of the sub- organizations due to their work for the Palestinian cause, and the legal hurdles the Brotherhood faced when raising funds for Hamas and other Palestinian causes or when taking orders from overseas leaders."[60] They also discussed what the ongoing role of ISNA[61] (the Islamic Society of North America) would be and how to conceal its activities from the U.S. government. "Palestine Committee members discussed the possibility of using ISNA as official cover for their activities."[62]

As a result of the discussions in Philadelphia, the Palestine Committee amended its by-laws "and declared that an as-yet-unnamed organization was already in the early stage of creation, "operat[ing] through" the IAP. It was soon to "become an official organization for political work, and its

---

[58] "CAIR Executive Director Placed at HAMAS Meeting" Counterterrorism Blog. The Investigative Project, August 2, 2007. http://www.investigativeproject.org/282/cair-executive-director-placed-at-hamas-meeting

[59] Investigation to R. Richard Newcomb, Director, Office of Foreign Asset Control, Department of Treasury, November 5, 2001, Herein "FBI Action Memorandum dated Nov. 5, 2001," http://nefafoundation.org/miscellaneous/HLF/WatsonMemo.pdf.

[60] According to testimony in CAIR's appeal to remove its name from the list of unindicted co-conspirators in the Holy Land Foundation Trial Memorandum Opinion Order http://www.investigativeproject.org/documents/case_docs/1425.pdf

[61] Years later, in May 2007, the Justice Department would classify ISNA among entities "who are and/or were members of the US Muslim Brotherhood." https://www.investigativeproject.org/documents/case_docs/423.pdf

[62] Ibid

headquarters will be in Washington, *insha Allah.*"[63] The discussions about this new organization by the participants highlighted their concern about what role it should play in their developing program of civilization jihad, *i.e.*, whether it should be a political organization, a low profile fundraising operation, or something else entirely.

The Creation of CAIR – Hamas in Sheep's Clothing

It did not take long to find out. Eight months later, in June 1994, the Council on American-Islamic Relations (CAIR) was co-founded by Nihad Awad, Omar Ahmad, and Rafeeq Jaber. Its funding included a $5,000 donation, earmarked as 'seed money,' from the Holy Land Foundation[64], now a well-endowed operation in Richardson, Texas. (For more on Holy Land Foundation, see Part V.) CAIR was set up as a new front for Hamas in the United States (most likely to replace the now compromised IAP). Its first office was established, as promised, in Washington, DC. By June 1996, CAIR claimed to have 32 satellite offices throughout the United States. Since then, CAIR has acted as a foil, a screen, a forward guard, and a fundraiser for Hamas, and has become the self-proclaimed civil rights champion of American Muslims.

Nihad Awad's presence at the Philadelphia conference identified him as a prominent figure in the Hamas/Muslim Brotherhood network. After he assumed leadership of CAIR, his role was to lead the organization into the mainstream, by denying any affiliation with Hamas. Rather than presenting CAIR as another Muslim not-for-profit fundraising organization, Awad promoted CAIR as "America's largest Muslim civil liberties organization" and "a nonprofit, grassroots civil rights and advocacy organization."[65] This was a departure from earlier Brotherhood-spawned groups, and turned out to be a brilliant idea. It also elevated Awad to a senior role in the Muslim Brotherhood's American organization.

CAIR claims on its website to be "the Muslim NAACP,"[66] but there is little doubt that its underlying intentions are more closely aligned with the support of terrorism than with civil rights. Closely following the Brotherhood's program of 'civilization jihad', CAIR fulfills its mission through a well-designed agenda of non-violent economic, humanitarian, and political activity that enables it to function in the 'mainstream', even while it secretly supports the steady subversion of American society, all

---

[63] The Roots of CAIR's Intimidation Campaign" by Andrew C. McCarthy,. National Review, April 12, 2014. http://www.nationalreview.com/article/375620/roots-cairs-intimidation-campaign-andrew-c-mccarthy

[64] A contribution, they later denied, until they were presented with a photocopy of the check. See https://www.investigativeproject.org/documents/misc/110.pdf

[65] "CAIR at a Glance" https://www.cair.com/about-us/cair-at-a-glance.html

[66] Ibid

funded by massive local donations, collected from wealthy supporters within the U.S.

CAIR invites all American Muslims to bring their grievances about unfair, anti-Muslim practices, ill treatment, discrimination, harassment by non-Muslims, and any other grievance it perceives as "Islamophobia" to its offices for remediation. It encourages American Muslims to join the struggle to support the acceptance of Islamic law in the U.S. as an *alternative to American law*, and to consider CAIR the go-to place for legal action against those they perceive as adversaries against Islam. Its website declares that all this is done in the name of "protecting the civil rights of all Americans regardless of faith" because "civil rights advocacy is at the center of CAIR's work."[67] Its solutions, however, are all based on the Muslim perspective as it derives from Islamic law and would hardly provide a satisfactory resolution for a non-Muslim.

---

[67] "What We Do" https://www.cair.com/civil-rights/what-we-do.html

PART II

CIVILIZATION JIHAD – INFILTRATING AMERICA

Civilization jihad in the U.S. includes the infiltration of American institutions, including local, state, and federal government, faith communities, schools and universities, prisons, and the military. This is accomplished through political activity, lobbying at the highest levels, and currying favor from civic leaders, the policy and decision makers, from the local to the state and federal levels. It also includes the particular forms of pressure that CAIR puts on the American scene with its program of anti-Islamophobia activism. And it includes the various Muslim organizations that are becoming increasingly vocal, demanding more services and accommodations than ever in the workplace, schools, and public accommodations, such as taxis and airports.

FBI veteran and founder of Understanding the Threat John Guandolo says "the most prominent Islamic organizations in the United States are all controlled by the Muslim Brotherhood."[68] Like the Brotherhood, they cloak their support for Hamas and other terrorist groups in 'good works' and 'community service', but unlike the Brotherhood, they function under their own well-known, public names that include the Muslim Student Association (MSA), Islamic Society of North America (ISNA), North American Islamic Trust (NAIT), Muslim Arab Youth Association (MAYA), and many more (see partial lists in Appendices III and V).

The MSA was the first Brotherhood organization to be formally established in the U.S. It was founded in January 1963 by its members at the University of Illinois, Urbana-Champaign campus, for the purpose of "spreading Islam as students in North America."[69] Currently, the MSA claims to have has nearly 100 chapters on university campuses across the country.[70]

In a speech in Missouri in the 1980's, Zaid Naman, a US Muslim Brotherhood official, made the relationship between the MSA and the MB clear. He stated that, "as for recruitment in the ranks of the Movement [the MB], its main condition was that a brother must be active in the general activism in the MSA."

---

[68] "FBI: Muslim Brotherhood Deeply Rooted Inside U.S." World Net Daily, February 21, 2011. http://www.wnd.com/2011/02/266725/

[69] "John Guandolo Discusses The Muslim Brotherhood's Network in America, Attacks the Media" by Alex Nitzberg Accuracy in Media, May 17, 2017 "http://www.aim.org/aim-column/john-guandolo-discusses-the-muslim-brotherhoods-network-in-america-attacks-the-media/

[70] http://msanational.org/msa-map/

CAIR's Public Image and Credibility Campaign

From the beginning, CAIR portrayed itself as a moderate, mainstream, civil rights/advocacy organization, and was quickly accepted in Washington as the official voice of American Muslims. By 1996, CAIR officers had achieved such a high level of credibility that they were frequent guests at VIP events sponsored by the State Department and the White House.[71]

One notable supporter of Hamas was Abdurahman Alamoudi, for example, who moved quickly up the circles of influence until he was strategically placed as a frequent guest at the White House, the Pentagon, and the State Department.

Once in Washington, he found a champion in Grover Norquist,[72] who shepherded him around among the D.C. elite, right up to and including the Bill Clinton and George W. Bush White Houses, where he was a welcome guest.

In 1990, Alamoudi founded the American Muslim Council and became the organization's executive director. In 1991, he established the Defense Department's American Muslim Armed Forces and Veterans Affairs Council (AMAFVAC), which vetted and certified all the Muslim chaplains hired by the military. Alamoudi hand-picked the men who would serve in the chaplains' corps.

On the occasion of the commissioning of the Army's second Muslim chaplain, Lieutenant JG Monje Malak Abd al-Muta Ali Noel, Jr., Alamoudi said, "We have taken a long and patient process to bring this through." He spoke of his plan to cultivate others to strive for positions in the political system and law

enforcement: "We have a few city council members. We are grooming our young people to be politicians. We also want them to be policemen and FBI

---

[71] "Council on American-Islamic Relations" DiscovertheNetworks.com, November 14, 2016 http://www.discoverthenetworks.org/printgroupprofile.asp?grpid=6176

[72] Grover Norquist is a Republican activist and the head of Americans for Tax Reform, who has been the darling of the Republican establishment, but who has also been associated with known terrorists and Muslim Brotherhood front groups.. He has shepherded prominent Muslims into the offices of the highest political figures in Washington, including Abdurahman Alamoudi.

agents,"[73] he said. Among the other chaplains he selected was the al-Qaeda imam Anwar al-Awlaki.[74]

He was also named head of the Muslim Chaplain's program for federal prisons,[75] with ISNA selected as the official agency to vet and recommend candidates for the program. These were both significant assignments because they gave the Brotherhood exclusive authority to vet candidates, and access to new populations of both military personnel and prisoners for conversion to Islam and, in some cases, radicalization. Alamoudi was even asked to be a resource in the investigation of the Safa Group . This was the height of folly, as he himself was also a significant player in the group.

L to R: Vice President Al Gore, Abdourahman Alamoudi, and President Bill Clinton. 1994. (Photo: CAIR)

During the 1992 presidential election cycle, Alamoudi contributed to both the Democratic and Republican parties. When Bill Clinton won the election, Alamoudi increased his contributions to the Democratic Party, served the administration as an Islamic-affairs adviser, and was appointed a State Department "goodwill ambassador" to the Muslim world. In that capacity, Alamoudi was sent on six official trips to Muslim nations in the Middle East, paid for by taxpayer funds.[76]

---

[73] Abdulrahman Alamoudi - Head of American Muslim Council goes to jail for 23 years." Militant Islam Monitor, October 29, 2004.
http://www.militantislammonitor.org/article/id/306

[74] Ibid

[75] Alamoudi personally screened and selected the Muslim chaplains who were assigned to federal prisons, and who eventually played a significant part in in-prison indoctrinations and conversions.

[76] Ibid

In early 1999, Alamoudi provided some $20,000 in seed money (in checks drawn on a Saudi bank account) to help Norquist establish an organization called the Islamic Free Market Institute (or Islamic Institute).[77]

Despite the fact that he was a favorite of the White House and had complete access to the highest levels of power in the federal government, he publicly stated his support of Hamas and Hizb'allah, and the mission of Hamas/Muslim Brotherhood in America. In December 1996, Alamoudi told a conference of the IAP:

"I think if we were outside this country, we can say, 'Oh, Allah, destroy America,' but once we are here, our mission in this country is to change it. … You can be violent anywhere else but in America."[78]

And a year before 9/11, at a rally outside the White House, he roused the crowd with the words, "We are ALL supporters of Hamas. Allahu Akbar! … I am also a supporter of Hezbollah." Yet the administration continued to give him complete access to the highest levels of power in the federal government, and still considered him a 'moderate Muslim'. In 2002, FBI spokesman for Director Robert Mueller referred to his American Muslim Council (AMC) as the "the most mainstream Muslim group in the United States."[79]

In short, until his downfall, Alamoudi was considered, as the Washington Post wrote, "a pillar of the local Muslim community."[80] His influence in high places came to an abrupt end in 2004, when he was caught carrying $340,000 at Heathrow Airport in the U.K. en route to Syria as part of a plot to murder then-Crown Prince Abdullah of Saudi Arabia.[81] The plot was prepared under the direction of Libyan leader Muammar Qaddafi, who provided the funding. Although Alamoudi agreed to cooperate in the investigation in return for having the 31 other charges dropped the possible

---

[77] Abdurahman Alamoudi
http://www.discoverthenetworks.org/individualProfile.asp?indid=1311

[78] "Alamoudi: You can be violent anywhere else…" The Investigative Project on Terrorism. December 28, 1996. http://www.investigativeproject.org/261/alamoudi-you-can-be-violent-anywhere-else

[79] "The American Muslim Council:] 'Mainstream' Muslims?" by Daniel Pipes. ^New York Post, June, 2002. http://www.danielpipes.org/423/the-american-muslim-council-mainstream-muslims

[80] "Abdulrahman Alamoudi - Head of American Muslim Council goes to jail for 23 years" Militant Islam Monitor, October 29, 2014.
http://www.militantislammonitor.org/article/id/306

[81] "Muslim Activist Sentenced to 23 Years for Libya Contacts" by Jerry Markon. Washington Post, October 16, 2004. http://www.washingtonpost.com/wp-dyn/articles/A36718-2004Oct15.html

reduction of the 23-year sentence, and fines of $750,000, in the end, he received the maximum sentence and lost his U.S. citizenship.

Hamas in American Politics

In recent years, the Brotherhood has been able to increase its influence at every level of American government, winning office in public elections, and affecting policy in every area of American life. In 2006, Keith Ellison became the first Muslim to win a seat in Congress from his district in Minnesota, and he took his oath of office on the Quran. In late 2016, he became a candidate for head of the powerful Democratic National Committee, and although he did not win, he was immediately appointed to the Deputy DNC Chair, second only to the newly elected Chair, Tom Perez, making Ellison the second most powerful person in the Democrat Party. Ellison appears regularly as a keynote speaker at large Brotherhood front group events, including the annual MAS-ICNA (Muslim American Society-Islamic Circle of North America) conference in Chicago, IL.

Congressman Keith Ellison in front of the U.S. Capitol

Abdullah Hammoud was elected to the Michigan State legislature (District 15) from Dearborn, Michigan in 2016, and he too was sworn in on the Quran. The significance of this is often under-estimated or ignored. It makes sense, of course, that a Muslim would not want to take his oath on the Judeo-Christian Bible, but implicit in his taking the oath is that he will consider it his highest obligation to:

> *"support and defend the Constitution of the United States against all enemies, foreign and domestic; that I will bear true faith and allegiance to the same; that I take this obligation freely, without any mental reservation or purpose of evasion; and that I will well and faithfully discharge the duties of the office on which I am about to enter: So help me God."*[82]

The conflict that exists between this vow and the obligation of Muslims to consider Islamic Law (shariah) the highest legal authority is significant. It raises the question of which authority would be higher should a conflict arise between them, and whether it is even possible to serve two such masters without an impossible conflict.

---

[82] "Oaths of Office For Federal Officials"
http://uspolitics.about.com/od/usgovernment/a/oaths_of_office_4.htm

Moreover, Ellison has himself been linked to the Muslim American Society (MAS), a Virginia-based non-profit 501(C)(3) organization, founded in 1993 to act as the "overt arm of the Muslim Brotherhood in the United States."[83] (On its website, MAS describes itself simply as "a dynamic charitable, religious, social, cultural, and educational, organization" with "more than 50 chapters across the United States."[84]

MAS embraces the orthodox Islamic teachings of Brotherhood founder Hassan al-Banna, which its members consider "the closest reflection of how Islam should be in this life,"[85] and its officers, past and present, are activists in Islamic and Hamas-linked organizations including the Islamic Society of North America (ISNA), the Muslim Student Association (MSA), and the North American Islamic Trust (NAIT).[86] In 2014, MAS was among those listed as terrorist organizations by the United Arab Emirates.

In 2008, MAS paid $13,500 to cover the cost of Ellison's hajj to Mecca. But Keith Ellison is just one of a growing legion of Muslim activists who have risen to prominence in the senior ranks of politics. The imperative for Muslims to insert themselves into the very fabric of American society is stated clearly on page 4 of the 'Memorandum':

> *"Enablement of Islam in North America, meaning: establishing an effective and a stable Islamic Movement led by the Muslim Brotherhood which adopts Muslims' causes domestically and globally, and which works to expand the observant Muslim base, aims at unifying and directing Muslims' efforts, presents Islam as a civilization alternative, and supports the global Islamic State wherever it is."*

In all things, Hamas in the U.S. is an arm of the *Ikhwan*, as stated in Article Two of its Covenant, and supports this relationship in all of its facets:

> *"The Islamic Resistance Movement is one of the wings of Moslem Brotherhood in Palestine. Moslem Brotherhood Movement is a universal organization, which constitutes the largest Islamic movement in modern times. It is characterized by its deep understanding, accurate comprehension and its complete embrace of all Islamic concepts of all aspects of life, culture, creed, politics, economics, education, society, justice and judgment, the*

---

[83] According to federal prosecutors in 2007.

[84] Muslim American Society official webite, http://muslimamericansociety.org/support/

[85] "A Rare Look at Secretive Brotherhood in America," by Noreen S. Ahmed-Ullah , Sam Roe and Laurie Cohen, *Chicago Tribune*, September 19, 2004.

[86] "Muslim American Society: The Investigative Project On Terrorism Dossier" http://www.investigativeproject.org/documents/misc/85.pdf

spreading of Islam, education, art, information, science of the occult, and conversion to Islam." [87]

Although CAIR promotes itself as a civil rights champion for American Muslims, its origins in the Muslim Brotherhood are well documented. In 2008, during the Holy Land Foundation retrial, CAIR was identified as "a front group for Hamas" in the testimony of an FBI special agent, and named an unindicted co-conspirator, along with two of its officers. Two years later, a federal judge ruled that there was "ample evidence" to prove that CAIR was a part of "a conspiracy to support Hamas."[88]

In November 2014, the United Arab Emirates (UAE) designated CAIR and the Muslim Association of America (another Muslim Brotherhood creation) among 83 terrorist organizations. While CAIR called this move "bizarre," and the Obama administration made efforts to reverse the designations, the UAE reiterated its decision, because of the connections that CAIR and MAS have to the Muslim Brotherhood, and because they promote "incitement or [terror] funding."[89]

Nevertheless, in the U.S., CAIR is still considered a credible representative and protector of American Muslims, in conjunction with a well-established network of mosques and 'community centers' around the country. Its mission to support the terrorist agenda of Hamas in the Middle East and promote civilization jihad in America continues unabated. CAIR carries out its American jihad through a program of attacking 'Islamophobia' for even the smallest 'slights', promoting the adoption of shariah law in America, and infiltrating American society at every level.

The Hamas/CAIR/Muslim Brotherhood Nexus

Since the Holy Land Foundation trial (see Part III), Muslim organizations have made a concerted effort to avoid calling attention to their fundraising activities, except for those directly related to projects in America. In order to do so, Hamas has carved out an ambitious program of strategies and tactics that support its dual mission in a potentially hostile

---

[87] Hamas Covenant, Article 2

[88] "FBI Document Depicting Relationship Between CAIR and Terror Group Hamas Published" Police Magazine, December 17, 2015. ·
http://www.policemag.com/channel/patrol/news/2015/12/17/fbi-document-depicting-relationship-between-cair-and-terror-group-hamas-published.aspx

[89] UAE Foreign Affairs Minister Sheikh Abdullah bin Zayed Al-Nahyan explained the specific designations of CAIR and MAS as terrorists during a television interview: "We cannot accept incitement or [terror] funding when we look at some of these organizations. For many countries, the definition of terror is that you have to carry a weapon and terrorize people. For us, it's far beyond that. We cannot tolerate even the smallest and tiniest amount of terrorism." Source: Clarion Project, November 26, 2014. https://clarionproject.org/uae-doubles-down-designation-cair-terrorists/

environment, and, as before, the boundaries between Hamas and other jihadist organizations are blurred and fluid. Like its counterpart in Gaza, CAIR uses an approach that creates the illusion of carrying out a targeted mission of providing social services and humanitarian support for Muslims in the United States. But where Hamas in Gaza's other face uses mortars, bombs, and tunnels to sow its seeds of terror, Hamas/CAIR in the U.S. focuses its attention on political activism and an aggressive program of subversion on Capitol Hill and throughout American society across the country.

Following the Holy Land Trial (see Part III), the Brotherhood in the U.S. has likely found other methods to channel funds outside of the U.S. in support of Hamas and other terrorist organizations. CAIR (like other U.S.-based Muslim Brotherhood front groups) has backed away from any overt connections with fundraising for terrorist-connected groups. It now limits its public fundraising activities to its own local (and very generous) donor network and distances itself from the funding of any Islamic Movement projects outside of the U.S.

Nevertheless, the chain of support for Hamas activities in other parts of the world have not been completely broken, particularly in the Palestinian territories in the West Bank, where local charities are recipients of both official aid from USAID and private support from charitable American organizations. One example is the Unlimited Friends Association for Social Development (UFA), which receives financial support from "at least eight prominent U.S. charities and, apparently, the taxpayer-funded United States Agency for International Development (USAID)."[90]

UFA operates in Gaza with the consent and cooperation of Hamas officials. At a 2014 ceremony, for example, which it organized to support the "right of return"[91] for Palestinians, the guest of honor was Hamas minister Mustafa Sawwaf, who once claimed that "Israel's disappearance is a necessity [according to] the Koran — that is a truth that we have learned and that we have been teaching since the first intifada, which was the

---

[90] How American Charities Fund Terrorism" by Sam Westrop. NationalReview.com, January 12, 2017. http://www.nationalreview.com/article/443773/terrorist-groups-american-charities-fund-ufa-hamas-dawah-social-services.

[91] Approximately 750,000 Palestinians were displaced in Israel's 1948 War of Independence (which Palestinians call 'nakba' or 'catastrophe'). Rather than being assimilated into the countries to which they fled, they became refugees who were never allowed to become absorbed into their new communities. Instead they were crowded into 58 UN-controlled 'refugee camps' in several Arab countries, where their numbers grew exponentially. Today there are more than 5 million descendants of the original Palestinian refugees scattered around the world who are recognized by the U.N. (https://www.unrwa.org/palestine-refugees) and who demand the "right of return" to what is now Israel. There is no historical precedent for descendants of refugees being also considered refugees. Since Israel's entire population is only slightly more than 8 million, this argument for a "right of return" is a non-starter for Israel on all counts.

Palestinian people's first step toward ending the usurpation of Palestine by the Jewish gangs."[92]

Other mechanisms for the secret transfer of funds are also still in play. The well-known *hawala* system is one such means through which small, untraceable transactions may still be funneling money abroad using services such as PayPal and TransferWise[93] in order to avoid disclosure. It is likely that U.S.-originated funds may, in such ways, find their way to Hamas or other Brotherhood entities abroad. As recently as 2016, Jonathan Schanzer reported that despite denials, the confluence of AMP, BDS, former officers of HLF, and AJP and the transfer of funds among them, are troubling, to say the least. He said, "There appear to be flaws in the federal and state oversight of non-profits charities."[94]

A New Strategy? The Pillars Fund

One interesting development in Islamic funding was reported in early September 2017, with the creation of Chicago-based Pillars Fund, a Muslim charitable fund that states on its website the basis of its mission:

> *"Pillars believes knowledge and dissemination of information by and about American Muslims can help mitigate implicit and explicit bias and promote a more just and inclusive society. We help institutions understand the critical role Muslims play in civil society and help them identify opportunities to be more thoughtful in their engagement with Muslims. Meaningful representation matters, especially when it comes to decisions and depictions that directly impact our communities. Since 2010, Pillars has advised the country's premier foundations, think tanks, civic leaders, filmmakers, and activists on how to use their distinct platforms to engage American Muslims."[95]*

Since its founding, Pillars reports on its website that it has invested "over $2 million in opportunities for American Muslim." Its emphasis on community 'understanding' and "dissemination of information by and about American Muslims" certainly seems to rise above the aggressive

---

[92] How American Charities Fund Terrorism" by Sam Westrop. NationalReview.com, January 12, 2017. http://www.nationalreview.com/article/443773/terrorist-groups-american-charities-fund-ufa-hamas-dawah-social-services.

[93] "Facebook's first funder just backed TransferWise, a startup that's like an ancient Islamic money transfer system" by Leo Morani. Qz.com. May 14, 2013 https://qz.com/84388/facebooks-first-funder-just-put-his-money-into-a-start-up-thats-a-lot-like-an-ancient-islamic-money-transfer-system/

[94] "Ties between Hamas-linked charities and BDS highlighted in Congressional testimony" by Rebecca Shimoni Stoil. *Israel Times*, April 20, 2016. http://www.timesofisrael.com/congressional-testimony-highlights-ties-between-hamas-linked-charities-bds/

[95] https://pillarsfund.org

discourse that currently colors the American scene. But a closer look at the Pillars website suggests the possibility of a deeper agenda.

One of the two leaders of the fund is Kalia Abiade, Director of Programs, whose history includes a stint as Advocacy Director at the Center for New Community in Chicago. In that capacity, she provided training for a program called, "How To Marginalize Your Opponents While Uplifting Your Values," targeting "organized racist movements [who] use sophisticated messaging platforms to advance their bigoted agenda."

In April 2017, Palestinian Legal retweeted one of Abiade's tweets: "2 be effective we MUST see connecting between policing, Islamophobia, support for Israeli repression to be effective" linking police, Islamophobia, and Israel and naming them as the enemy." This sounds less like an attempt to "mitigate implicit and explicit bias and promote a more just and inclusive society" than a dark proposal to delegitimize those with whom the author disagrees, linking law enforcement, the all-encompassing epithet of "Islamophobia," and everything relating to Israel in one hateful message. Yet the author is co-leader of the organization whose home page (pillarsfund.org) proclaims its own mission statement: "There is no 'us' and 'them' in the American identity, only an evolving 'we'." In this case, however, the "we" to which it refers excludes policemen, "Islamophobes," and anyone associated with Israel.

Another familiar name among the members of the Board of Advisors is Linda Sarsour (see Part V: "Other Enablers of the Muslim Brotherhood's Civilization Jihad Agenda"), whose blatant anti-Semitism and phony feminism make her leadership within the "civil rights" movement of 2017 a dangerous hoax. With such leadership, it is not difficult to imagine that Pillars has a deeper agenda than what appears so innocently on its website.

Like other organizations described in this volume, Pillars appears to be a benign charitable organization, while masking a deeper agenda that is in line with the Muslim Brotherhood's master plan to create a Muslim country in America.

The relationships the Hamas/CAIR/Muslim Brotherhood nexus has forged since 1987 have blossomed into full-blown programs of alliances plus a multitude of front groups, all dedicated to their dual mission in the Middle East and the U.S. The boundaries between the organi-zations are so blurred that it is difficult to know where one ends and the other begins. But from the maze of connected groups that make up their network, there emerges an insidious and even seditious action plan that puts America and the core principles upon which it was founded at high risk.

In its most blatant form, members and supporters simply deny the existence of the Brotherhood and Hamas in the U.S. An example of this was demonstrated by Suhail A. Khan, former Bush administration official and gatekeeper to the Muslim community for the President. He was invited to speak at the annual Conservative Political Action Conference (CPAC) meeting in Washington in February 2011, where he stated, "There's no Muslim Brotherhood in the United States."[96]

He reiterated this statement later on Fox News' Sean Hannity show[97] in a confrontation with Frank Gaffney, CEO of the Center for Strategic Policy[98] and David Horowitz, founder and president of the Freedom Center.[99] When pressed by Hannity on the subject, he said, "I'm a conservative activist who focuses on conservative issues. If there is a Muslim Brotherhood, I'm not aware of it. You know, to my knowledge, there is no official presence of the Muslim Brotherhood in this country."

True to the tradition of Muslim Brotherhood's pattern of double speak, aside from the key qualifier of 'official presence,' his statement was patently false and he knew it. It was a classic example of *taqiyya*, lying to the *kufar*[100] for the sake of Islam.

Suhail Khan's background is revealing. In his public persona, Khan calls himself a Conservative Reagan Republican. But in a less public forum, he is deeply connected to the Islamic movement in America. His name has been linked to Abdurahman Alamoudi and Sami al-Arian.[101]

His father, the late Mahboob Khan, was a founding member of the Muslim Student Association (MSA), the Islamic Society of North America (ISNA), the Muslim Community Association (MCA), and American Muslims for Global Peace and Justice. All of these organizations were created by and fall under the protection of the Muslim Brotherhood. Suhail Khan has

---

[96] https://www.youtube.com/watch?v=_a38lTKNhgw

[97] The Sean Hannity Show, February 15, 2011.

[98] www.centerforsecuritypolicy.org/

[99] "Who Is Sukhail Khan?" by Paul Sperry, January 19, 2011
http://www.frontpagemag.com/fpm/82238/who-suhail-khan-paul-sperry

[100] *Kufar is* the Arabic word meaning "unbelievers" or "non-Muslims." The term refers to those who reject (or does not follow) the teachings of Mohammed and does not accept Islam as their faith.

[101] Sami al-Arian was a tenured University of South Florida computer science professor, who founded the Islamic Committee for Palestine, once called "the active arm of the Islamic Jihad movement in Palestine." Al-Arian also founded the World and Islam Studies Enterprise (WISE), an Islamic think tank that ostensibly worked with a USF faculty group to organize seminars and share libraries. Al-Arian also served as secretary to the Palestinian Islamic Jihad (PIJ), a terrorist group . Following a 1995 terrorist bombing in which 19 Israelis were murdered, he wrote, "The latest operation, carried out by the two *mujahideen* (Islamic guerilla fighters) who were martyred for the sake of God, is the best guide and witness to what they believing few can do in the face of Arab and Islamic collapse at the heels of the Zionist enemy..." Years earlier he said, "This is the way of giving," he said earlier. "This is the way of struggle. This is the way of battle. This is the way of jihad. This is the way of martyrdom. Thus is the way of blood, because this is the path to heaven." He was indicted on 17 counts of aiding terrorism in February 2003 and, following a plea bargain, was deported to Turkey in 2015.

vowed to carry on his "dear father's shining legacy." [102] Khan's mother, Malika Khan, was also a founding member of the MCA and is currently a board member of the Council on American-Islamic Relations' (CAIR) California chapter.

It stretches the bounds of credibility to believe that Suhail Khan had no idea of the Brotherhood's relationship to all these organizations. To say that there is no Muslim Brotherhood in America denies his own family heritage.

But the deep connections of his family members to Muslim organizations spawned and controlled by the Muslim Brotherhood tell only part of the story. Suhail himself revealed his true Muslim convictions in a 1999 speech to ISNA, when he said:

> *"The earliest defenders of Islam would defend their more numerous and better equipped oppressors, because the early Muslims loved death, dying for the sake of almighty Allah, more than the oppressors of Muslims loved life. This must be the case where we-- when we are fighting life's other battles. ... [W]hat are our oppressors going to do with people like us? We're prepared to give our lives for the cause of Islam."[103]*

This is the language of jihad, and Khan[104] has shown himself again and again to be an excellent practitioner of *taqiyya*. Khan continues to be active – both in Washington political circles and in Muslim affairs.

Hamas' success in the U.S. has depended heavily upon fluid but fuzzy connections with other terrorist organizations that help it maintain its cloak of secrecy. It has also depended on high value financiers affiliated with and sympathetic to the world of terrorism.

In studying the complex network of interconnecting organizations and individuals, it is difficult to avoid the conclusion that the alliance between Hamas and the Muslim Brotherhood in the U.S. is very close, and that identifying clear paths of individual activity and involvement is extremely difficult. Although many of the Muslim Brotherhood organizations openly support Hamas activities and groups, provide legal assistance when necessary, and may still be raising funds for them (something they will deny), the overall illusion is that Hamas doesn't exist in America at all. This is an integral part of the scheme to confuse and deceive.

Given the vast amount of documentation, however, the inescapable conclusion is that Hamas *is* the Muslim Brotherhood and that it operates secretly in the U.S. under the protective mantle of CAIR, its public persona.

---

[102] Obituary: Mahboob Khan. Islamic Voice, May 1999.
http://www.islamicvoice.com/may.99/COMMUNity.HTM

[103] Ibid

[104] Obituary: Mahboob Khan. The Islamic Voice, May 1999.
http://suhailkhanexposed.com/wp-content/uploads/2011/02/MB_Case_Study_Evidence.pdf

The Hamas/CAIR/Muslim Brotherhood nexus is not only active here in the U.S., it is pursuing its goals aggressively to support its program of Hamas terror in the Middle East and Civilization Jihad in the United States.

PART III

SUPPORTING HAMAS – RAISING MONEY FOR TERROR

The Holy Land Foundation

The story of the Holy Land Foundation (HLF), which was the largest Islamic charity in the U.S. until it was shut down in December 2001, illustrates the effectiveness of the Brotherhood's vast network and explains Hamas' great interest in its success. In its early days, the Holy Land Foundation was called the Occupied Land Fund (OLF), under which name it operated and shared checking accounts with the Islamic Society of North America (ISNA).

Operating under its new name and headquartered in Richardson, Texas, the HLF became central to the Hamas fundraising efforts in the U.S. It served as a clearing-house for millions of dollars in *zakat* (the annual obligatory tax on all shariah-compliant Muslims and Muslim businesses, a percentage of which is designated for jihad). The money made its way through a network of covert channels to Hamas and the Palestinian Islamic Jihad (PIJ). Funds raised by the Holy Land Foundation were used by Hamas to support terrorist actions against Israel, in addition to funding programs which indoctrinated children to become suicide bombers, to recruit teenagers and adults to violent jihad, and to support their families after they died or went to prison.

From 2007-2008, the U.S. Treasury prosecuted HLF on over one hundred counts of material support to terrorism. 50 U.S. Code § 1701[105] explicitly spells out the criteria on which this prosecution was based. These include any "unusual and extraordinary threat, which has its source in whole or substantial part outside the United States, to the national security, foreign policy, or economy of the United States, if the President declares a national emergency with respect to such threat."[106]

Accordingly, on January 23, 1995, President Bill Clinton issued Executive Order (E.O.) 12947, "Prohibiting Transactions With Terrorists Who Threaten To Disrupt the Middle East Peace Process."[107] A 2016 article

---

[105] "50 U.S. Code § 1701 - Unusual and extraordinary threat; declaration of national emergency; exercise of Presidential authorities"
https://www.law.cornell.edu/uscode/text/50/1701

[106] Ibid

[107] "Executive Order 12947—Prohibiting Transactions With Terrorists Who Threaten To Disrupt the Middle East Peace Process" https://www.treasury.gov/resource-center/sanctions/Documents/12947.pdf

published by the Center for Security Policy, spelled out the criteria on which the lawsuit was based:

> *"In 2008, the United States Department of Justice successfully prosecuted the Holy Land Foundation for Relief and Development (HLF) and its founders on 108 charges, including material support for terrorism, money laundering and tax fraud. The government's theory of the case, successfully proven at trial, was that the Holy Land Foundation was established as a front group of the Palestine Committee—a covert organization of the U.S. branch of the Muslim Brotherhood—and that its purpose in this conspiracy was to provide funds for the Palestinian terrorist organization, Hamas."[108]*

The story of the fall of the Holy Land Foundation began in 2002. The organization was charged, and was convicted a year later, of smuggling money to Hamas through Panama and the Channel Islands[109]. The strict banking secrecy laws that characterized these off-shore banking havens protected the money that flowed through them and enabled Hamas to obscure both the origin and the destination of the money.[110]

The Holy Land Foundation trial became the largest terrorism financing prosecution in American history. In November 2008, the principals were found guilty on charges of providing material support to Hamas, a designated foreign terrorist organization, and with funneling $12.4 million to Hamas and Palestinian Islamic Jihad (PIJ) through its secret money-laundering channels.

One of the outcomes of the trial was the creation of a long list of unindicted co-conspirators in the Holy Land Foundation affair (see Appendix VI). Among those on the list were leaders of the Muslim Brotherhood in America and some of its organizations, such as ISNA, NAIT, and CAIR, that helped support Brotherhood efforts to fund Hamas.

In a 2008 memo to the U.S. District Court in Dallas, federal prosecutors wrote:

> *"ISNA and NAIT, in fact, shared more with HLF than just a parent organization [the Muslim Brotherhood]. They were intimately*

---

[108] "C.A.I.R. IS HAMAS: How the Federal Government Proved that the Council on American-Islamic Relations is a front for Terrorism." Center for Security Policy.
https://www.centerforsecuritypolicy.org/wp-content/uploads/2016/12/CAIR_is_HAMAS.pdf

[109] The Channel Islands are an archipelago in the English Channel off the French coast of Normandy that are known for offering a high level of security with tightly-controlled banking laws that provide cover for international money laundering.

[110] "Funds Under Terror Probe Flowed From Offshore" by Glenn R. Simpson, Staff Reporter of The Wall Street Journal, Updated March 22, 2002
http://www.wsj.com/articles/SB1016749797949129440

*connected with the HLF and its assigned task of providing
financial support to Hamas. ... Shortly after Hamas was founded
in 1987, as an outgrowth of the Muslim Brotherhood, the
International Muslim Brotherhood ordered the Muslim
Brotherhood chapters throughout the world to create Palestine
Committees, whose job it was to support Hamas with 'media,
money and men.'*

*"The U.S. Muslim Brotherhood created the U.S. Palestine
Committee, which documents reflect was initially comprised of
three organizations: the OLF (HLF), the IAP [Islamic Association
for Palestine], and the UASR [United Association for Studies and
Research]. CAIR was later added to these organizations."*[111]

Among the wealth of intelligence that emerged from the trial was the
revelation of the extent to which the Muslim Brotherhood either founded or
took control of the multitude of Muslim organizations in America. Money
came to the organization from *zakat* paid to organizations like the Islamic
Society of North America (ISNA) and the North American Islamic Trusts
(NAIT). Funds were then diverted to Hamas in Gaza and other jihadist
organizations through a variety of money-laundering channels. Hamas'
Secretary General, Khaled Mashaal, who was operating from Damascus,
Syria, relied on Mohammed el-Mezain, the HLF Chairman and Director of
Endowments to supervise the distribution of funds.[112] During the six years
between 1995-2001, HLF sent "approximately $12.4 million outside of the
United States with the intent to contribute funds, goods, and services to
Hamas."[113]

In the end, prosecutors concluded: "The mandate of these organizations, per
the International Muslim Brotherhood, was to support Hamas."

Changing Names, But Not Missions

In December 2001, the United States Customs Service (USCS), the
Internal Revenue Service - Criminal Investigation (IRS-CI), and the Federal
Bureau of Investigation (FBI) began an investigation of a number of people
suspected of providing material support for terrorist organizations, money
laundering, and tax evasion. Because they were thought to be using various
legitimate companies and charities as cover for these activities, no company
was completely safe from official scrutiny. Therefore, it became the
convention practiced by the Brotherhood that when an organization came

---

[111] http://www.wnd.com/2011/02/266725/#lqctTmfHpvQVI3fs.99

[112] According to 1993 tax documents IRS Form 990, filed by the Holy Land Foundation.

[113] https://www.treasury.gov/resource-center/terrorist-illicit-finance/Pages/protecting-
charities_execorder_13224-e.aspx

under too much scrutiny, or was forced to close, a new organization was formed to take over the work of the old one.

When the Holy Land Foundation was designated as the funding arm of Hamas, it was forced to close its funding channels as well as its doors. According to expert testimony by Jonathan Schanzer before the Subcommittees on Terrorism, Nonproliferation, and Trade, and the Middle East and North Africa in April 2016,[114] this did not stop its work.

Kindhearts for Charitable Humanitarian Development

The HLF's work continued through a new not-for-profit organization, called the Kindhearts for Charitable Humanitarian Development. Kindhearts, which was incorporated in 2002 in Toledo, Ohio, operated with a stated mission to provide "humanitarian aid without regard to religion or political affiliation."[115]

Kindhearts itself came under investigation by the U.S. Department of Justice in 2006, and the Treasury's Office of Foreign Assets Control (OFAC). On 19 February 2006, OFAC executed a search warrant on the Kindhearts headquarters as well as on the residence of its president Khaled Smaili. They seized all of its records, computers, equipment, and publications, and froze $1 ptechKindHearts assets.[116]

OFAC issued a press release[117] in which it outlined the reasons for its investigation. It reported that Kindhearts "coordinated with Hamas leaders and made contributions to Hamas-affiliated organizations," not only in Gaza but also in the West Bank and Lebanon.

According to the U.S. Treasury Department:

"Information developed from abroad corroborates connections between KindHearts and Hamas in Lebanon. As of late December 2003, KindHearts was supporting Hamas and other Salafi groups in the Palestinian refugee camps in Lebanon. [From 1998 -2000 Social Services Director for the HLF Haytham Maghawri] approved fifty wire transfers by the HLF in the amount of $407,512 USD, to nine zakat committees identified as being owned, controlled, or directed by Hamas.

---

[114] Testimony by Jonathan Schanzer, Vice President for Research at the Foundation for Defense of Democracies and former terror finance analyst for the US Treasury

[115] "Kindhearts Case Timeline" Charity and Security Network July 9. 2010. http://www.charityandsecurity.org/litigation/KindHearts_Timeline

[116] Ibid

[117] "Treasury Freezes Assets of Organization Tied to Hamas." U.S. Department of the Treasury, 2/19/2006. https://www.treasury.gov/press-center/press-releases/Pages/js4058.aspx

> *"According to the information source from abroad, KindHearts began working secretly and independently in the camps in Lebanon after the closure of the offices of the Sanabil Association for Relief and Development (Sanabil), a Hamas-affiliated entity in Lebanon . . . . In early 2003, KindHearts president Smaili complained that scrutiny by U.S. law enforcement and intelligence officials was making it almost impossible for KindHearts to assist Hamas.*
>
> *"Between July and December 2002, KindHearts sent more than $100,000 USD to the Lebanon-based SDGT Sanabil, according to information available to the U.S. Financial investigation revealed that between February 2003 and July 2003, KindHearts transferred over $150,000 USD to Sanabil. KindHearts deposited the funds into the same account used by HLF when it was providing funds to the Hamas-affiliated Sanabil, according to FBI analysis."[118]*

Khalid Mashaal had instructed that all financial contributions to Hamas from individuals in America should be funneled through el-Mezain,[119] who coordinated all of the KindHearts' fundraising activities, although El-Mezain had himself been indicted by the federal grand jury in Dallas, Texas, on charges of providing material support to Hamas in the Holy Land trial.

The OFAC press release asserted that KindHearts was founded to replace the Hamas-affiliated Holy Land Foundation for Relief and Development [HLF] and the al-Qaida-affiliated Global Relief Foundations [GRF]. This began a long legal wrangle that lasted until 2012. KindHearts was forced to close, but the court decided that the manner in which the Treasury had shut it down while investigating its alleged ties to terrorism had violated the Constitution.[120] It therefore allowed Kindhearts to distribute the remaining $1 million of its assets to first pay off its debts and to then to allocate the remaining balance among a list of approved charities, before it closed its operations for good.

American Muslims for Palestine (AMP)

Just as the Holy Land Foundation had morphed into Kindhearts, Kindhearts itself had to be reinvented when it was forced to close. While members of the HLF leadership were jailed, many of its personnel found

---

[118] https://www.treasury.gov/resource-center/terrorist-illicit-finance/Pages/protecting-charities_execorder_13224-e.aspx

[119] Ibid

[120] "Kindhearts Case Timeline" Idem.

jobs in a new organization called American Muslims for Palestine (AMP). The Chicago-based organization, that shares offices with the Americans for Justice in Palestine (AJP), is today a leading driver of the Hamas-linked Boycott, Divest, and Sanction (BDS) organization, and a sponsor and organizer for Students for Justice in Palestine (SJP).

Schanzer confirmed that the leaders of Kindhearts "gravitated to a new organization called American Muslims for Palestine (AMP)." He further testified that he had tracked employees of three now-defunct organizations — the Holy Land Foundation for Relief and Development, Kind Hearts Foundation for Humanitarian Development, and the Islamic Association for Palestine — all of which had been implicated in the financial support of Hamas.

Schanzer testified that "at least seven individuals who work for or on behalf of AMP have worked for or on behalf of organizations previously shut down or held civilly liable in the United States for providing financial support to Hamas: the Holy Land Foundation (HLF), Islamic Association for Palestine (IAP), and KindHearts."[121]

---

[121] "Former Treasury Official: Same Network That Funded Hamas in U.S. Backs Boycotts of Israel" by TheTower.org Staff | April 20, 2016 http://www.thetower.org/3260oc-former-treasury-official-same-network-that-funded-hamas-in-u-s-backs-boycotts-of-israel/

PART IV

Northern Virginia: A Haven for the Hamas/CAIR/Muslim Brotherhood Nexus

The Safa Group and the SAAR Foundation

The raid on the Herndon community in 2002 uncovered a huge organization of Hamas-related activity, camouflaged as community leaders, legitimate companies, and not-for-profit organizations. Known as the Safa Group, it was a complex network of more than one hundred front organizations that laundered money destined for Hamas operations in Gaza.

In a report on the status of the links between charitable organizations and terrorist financing, Matthew Levitt wrote, "The long list of charitable and business front organizations run out of 555 Grove Street in Herndon, Virginia, demonstrates[s] the critical need to break away from the tendency to adhere to a strict compartmentalization of terrorist groups in investigating terrorism cases."[122]

A dense maze of layered, interconnected organizations was created that became, as it continued to grow, increasingly difficult to untangle. The Hamas-linked groups, operating under the invisible umbrella of the Muslim Brotherhood, were able to function in relative freedom. Having adopted the face of benign acceptance of the American way of life, the Hamas/CAIR/Muslim Brotherhood network was secretly building out its network and infiltrating America's institutions. Its members joined university faculties, entered local governments, sat on local school boards, ran for local, state, and federal office, and, in short, hid themselves in plain sight behind the protective coloring of 'legitimate' businesses, 'charitable' organizations, and public service.

After 1997, when the US State Department included Hamas on its list of "Designated Foreign Terrorist Organizations"[123], the subterfuge became

---

[122] "Charitable Organizations and Terrorist Financing: A War on Terror Status-Check" by Matthew Levitt. Washington Institute, March 19, 2004.
http://www.washingtoninstitute.org/policy-analysis/view/charitable-organizations-and-terrorist-financing-a-war-on-terror-status-che

[123] According to the State Department notes, "Foreign Terrorist Organizations (FTOs) are foreign organizations that are designated by the Secretary of State in accordance with section 219 of the Immigration and Nationality Act (INA), as amended. FTO designations play a critical role in our fight against terrorism and are an effective means of curtailing support for terrorist activities and pressuring groups to get out of the terrorism business."
http://www.state.gov/j/ct/rls/other/des/123085.htm

increasingly urgent. But the designation did little to slow down the activities of the shadow companies and not-for-profits that hid much of the Brotherhood's funding support for Hamas through its U.S. organizations. Although Hamas was covertly headquartered in Herndon, Virginia, its network extended throughout the U.S., hiding its fund-raising and money-laundering operations behind more than 110 'legitimate' operations, some of which, according to court documents, existed only on paper.[124]

The Safa Group network was comprised of more than 100 companies, charities, educational institutes, and cultural organizations, most of which had their offices in a small neighborhood in Herndon, Virginia. In the federal investigation, a number of individuals were singled out for scrutiny. These included Taha Jaber al-Alwani, Jamal Barzinji, Yaqub Mirza, M. Omar Ashraf, Ahmad Totonji, Iqbal Unus, Muhammed Jaghlit, and his brother, M. Omar Ashraf. Many of those were singled out because they held multiple positions in the scores of companies that comprised the Safa Group.

In an affidavit deposed in March 2002, United States Customs Service (USCS) Special Agent David Kane declared that Safa Group organizations and the individuals associated with them were engaged in a criminal conspiracy "to provide material support to terrorist organizations by a group of Middle Eastern nationals living in Northern Virginia."[125] Kane's purpose was to show "probable cause" that the individuals named conspired to move funds internationally to promote "offenses against foreign nations involving murder . . . explosives, fire, kidnapping or extortion" in violation of U.S law. He further stated that they provided "material support or resources to foreign terrorist organizations," that they concealed or disguised "the source of ownership of material support intended for use in preparation for or in carrying out a terrorist act."[126]

Jonathan Schanzer testified that these individuals and organizations conspired against the United States through tax fraud, including the filing of false tax-exempt forms. Kane reported that the organizations associated with the Safa group were "suspected of providing support to terrorists, money laundering, and tax evasion through the use of a variety of for-profit

---

[124] "Muslim Anger Burns Over Lingering Probe of Charities" by Jerry Markon. *Washington Post,* October 11, 2006 http://www.washingtonpost.com/wp-dyn/content/article/2006/10/10/AR2006101001234.html

[125] "Affidavit in Support of Application for Search Warrant in the Matter of Searches Involving 555 Grove Street, Herndon, Virginia, and Related Locations." District Court for the Eastern District of Virginia.

[126] 18 U.S. Code § 2339A - Providing material support to terrorists. https://www.law.cornell.edu/uscode/text/18/2339A

companies and ostensible charitable entities under their control, most of which are located at 555 Grove Street, Herndon, VA."[127]

The scheme was complex and the affidavit was 107 pages long. It traced the transfer of funds from the Safa Group organizations "directly to terrorist-front organizations" back to the early 1990s. Kane testified that it involved such high profile cases as the trial of Sami al-Arian , a University of South Florida professor "who fronted for the Palestinian Islamic Jihad – Shikaki Faction,"[128] and was indicted for being the group's leader and chief financier in North America. PIJ was formally designated a terrorist organization in 1995, and al-Arian was deported to Turkey in 2015.

According to the affidavit, "the finances of the Safa Group . . . exhibited a convoluted web of multiple transactions between related corporations and charities that made it virtually impossible for federal investigators to ascertain where the money that finally left the web of the Safa Group ultimately went." In the end, the convoluted money trail traced millions of dollars to the Isle of Man, where the trail suddenly went cold because of the protective banking laws there.[129]

As a result, the Safa Group kept functioning, throughout the 1990s and into the twenty-first century. In reviewing the earlier investigation, Kane noted that, "the Safa Group engaged in the money laundering tactic of 'layering' to hide from la=nforcement authorities the trail of its support for terrorists. There appears to be no innocent explanation for the use of so many layers of transactions between Safa Group companies and charities *other* than to throw law enforcement authorities off the trail," he said.[130]

An example of how the system worked can be found in the operations of a company called Mar-Jac Poultry, a large *halal*[131] poultry processor in Gainesville, Georgia, and one of the Safa Group companies. Mar-Jac was accused by David Kane of transferring millions of dollars to companies and 'charities' within the Safa network. For example, Mar-Jac would loan money to charity A, then reassign the note to charity B, which would not collect on the loan. The money would then be transferred to another organization within the network, or to an off-shore bank, which would then make it available to Hamas or a Hamas-proxy, that would relay it on to the terrorist

---

[127] "Affidavit in Support of Application for Search Warrant in the Matter of Searches Involving 555 Grove Street, Herndon, Virginia, and Related Locations." District Court for the Eastern District of Virginia.

[128] Ibid

[129] Ibid

[130] Ibid

[131] The Arabic word 'halal' means 'permissible' or 'lawful'. The rules governing the slaughter and preparation of halal food are based on the Muslim rules under shariah law. The opposite of 'halal' is 'haram', which translates to 'forbidden' or 'unlawful' under shariah.

group. The greater the number of transactions, the greater the number of layers in the process, the more difficult it was to track the money.[132]

The list of companies in the Safa group contained real estate management, investment, educational, food, and other types of companies as well as not-for-profit companies, foundations, and Islamic organizations. Their role was to raise money through the solicitation of charitable contributions and legitimate business operations and channel the money to the Hamas organization in Gaza without calling attention to their own participation in this complex scheme. If one company became suspect, it was closed and morphed into a new organization under a new name, which continued the process.

The affidavit charged that there was probable cause to suspect that money transferred to the scores of Safa Group organizations by Mar-Jac was ultimately forwarded to Hamas and Palestinian Islamic Jihad-Shikaki Faction, both federally designated terrorist groups.[133]

The organizations within the Safa Group would "transfer large amounts of funds between each other" as a matter of course, leaving funds in any account for only a short period of time before transferring them on to other accounts. Such so-called "pass through" accounts are "commonly utilized by criminal organizations to convolute the trail of any illicit monies," the affidavit stated.

Mar-Jac was owned by principals of the Safa Group and, despite the explicit findings of the investigation, is still operational. Today, it employs more than 1,200 people at its Gainesville plant, which at peak capacity can process some 20,000 chickens per hour. The officers of Mar-Jac still include some of the principals of the old Safa Group in Virginia, as corporation records filed with the Georgia secretary of state show. For example, the chief executive officer, Jamal Barzinji, is listed as a director or principal on a dozen of Safa Group charities and companies that were also under investigation at the time. Yaqub Mirza, the company's secretary, is listed on 29 other Safa Group companies and organizations. The homes of both men were searched by the government in the March 2002 raid.

According to the affidavit:

"Kane used Mar-Jac Poultry as an example of such activity in his affidavit. Bank records for a Safa Group organization called the Sterling Charitable Gift Fund showed that it deposited a check from Mar-Jac Poultry in the amount of $250,000 on Oct. 26, 2001, according to Kane's affidavit. Sterling's bank records show that

---

[132] "Affidavit In Support Of Application For Search Warrant (October 2003)"
https://www.investigativeproject.org/documents/case_docs/891.pdf

[133] "Affidavit traces financial probe of Georgia poultry firm" by Rebecca Carr. The Atlanta Journal-Constitution November 17, 2003.
http://www.ajc.com/news/content/news/1103/17terror.html

Another organization operating out of the northern Virginia was the United Association for Studies and Research (UASR), which presented itself as a think tank. It published an academic journal, but prosecutors say it was also "involved in passing Hamas communiqués to the United States-based Muslim Brotherhood community and relaying messages from that community back to Hamas."[136]

Yaqub Mirza

In reviewing the management of the Safa Group companies and organizations, it is interesting to see how many of them list the same officers, sometime with deviations in spellings, some of whom have also been linked to close support of Hamas terrorist activities. For example, Muhamad Ashraf is listed as an officer or registered agent of 29 different companies and not-for-profit organizations on the Safa Group list. He is also among the individuals cited as unindicted co-conspirators in the Holy Land Foundation trial.

Yaqub M. Mirza is also listed as a senior officer or registered agent or both for at least 29 different organizations operating within the Safa Group. In March 2002, he was investigated by the FBI for possible ties with several terrorist groups and individuals, including Palestinian Islamic Jihad, Hamas, al Qaeda, Abdul Aziz Odeh, Omar Abdel Rahman, and Osama bin Laden.

The SAAR Foundation

At the heart of the investigation was the SAAR Foundation, another not-for-profit organization associated with the Safa Group and run by Yaqub Mirza. Established in the 1970s by Saudi Sheikh Sulaiman Abdul Aziz Rajihi (after whom it was named), its mission was ostensibly to help "scholars and scientists from the Middle East and Asia to create charitable

---

[134] Ibid

[135] Recent information indicates that the US halal industry is being tapped for funding of US-based mosque/Islamic Center projects, an apparent focus on keeping that money inside the US.

[136] Selected Government Exhibits & Documents from U.S. v. Holy Land Foundation
http://www.nefafoundation.org/hlfdocs/

programs that would supply food, education, and technology to Islamic countries."[137]

The FBI and the U.S. Customs agency, however, suspected that it was set up to raise and launder money for international terrorist groups like Hamas. Because its offices were located in the Safa Group compound at 555 Grove Street in Herndon, Virginia, the SAAR Foundation had every opportunity to develop and maintain close relationships with other Safa group companies and organizations. Among the highest-profile person who was associated with the SAAR Foundation was Abdurrahman Alamoudi, who served as its executive assistant to the president in northern Virginia from 1985 to 1990.

In 1998, the SAAR Foundation 'donated' $9 million to a Channel Islands entity called the Humana Charitable Trust, registered on the Isle of Man. In the same year, it also reported a $231,000 debt to Key Overseas Inc., a Panamanian company. Hamas accomplished its transfers through accommodating banks in various parts of the world. These banks either turned a blind eye to the illegal transactions or, like al-Taqwa Bank, were sympathizers to the cause and participants in the transfer process.

Money was also transferred to Hamas through a process known as *hawala,* a shariah-driven, paperless process used extensively by the global Muslim community to move funds across international boundaries without leaving a documented money trail. In developing their money-laundering channels, the Safa Group and the SAAR Foundation became the standard for Hamas funding in the West. The interchangeability of organizations in this massive money-laundering scheme was key to the success of the SAAR Foundation and the Safa Group, and kept its activity out of the limelight for quite a long time.

But this house of cards came tumbling down in March 2002, when the FBI and U.S. Customs raided the Safa Group's offices in Herndon, as well as the homes of some of its officers, and seized its records. According to David Kane's affidavit, the FBI was authorized to carry out a search of Mirza's offices as well as his home in Herndon.[138]

The Raid on the Safa Group

In March 2002, federal agents raided Safa's Virginia offices in more than fifteen locations in Falls Church, Leesburg, Herndon, and throughout Fairfax County. They seized computers and boxes of documents that included financial records, mailing lists, and the names and information of staff members. Among the other homes raided were those of Omar Ashraf,

---

[137] http://www.investigativeproject.org/activities/310/saar-network

[138] Ibid

Muhammed Ashraf, and Iqbal Unus, all associated with the Safa Group's All Dulles Area Muslim Society (ADAMS) Center.[139]

The information obtained in this raid supported the allegations of a pattern of complex transactions by the Safa Group that were designed to confuse law-enforcement authorities and keep them off the money trail. One U.S. official who was involved in the ensuing investigation said of the Safa network, "Looking at their finances is like looking into a black hole."[140]

According to David Kane's affidavit, the Safa Group's leadership intended "to route money through hidden paths to terrorists, and to defraud the United States by impeding, importing, obstructing, and defeating the lawful functions of the IRS."

> *"The information obtained in this raid revealed a pattern of multi-layered transactions by the SAFA Group that were designed to confuse law-enforcement authorities and keep them off the money trail. Of $54 million dollars raised by the SAAR Foundation ostensibly for "charity," $26 million went to the Isle of Man in the Irish Sea, a notorious location for drug runners and money laundering. Only $20 million made its way to SAFA Group charities."[141]*

The Safa Group remains a classic example of how the Muslim Brotherhood-linked organizations employ extreme and facile obfuscation in order to protect the secrecy of their operations, which were, at their core, designed to provide significant financial support to Hamas in the Middle East.

Boston, Massachusetts - A Magnet for Terrorists

Like Northern Virginia, Boston, Massachusetts has proven to be a safe haven for Hamas-linked activity, and the building of mosques, community centers, and charitable enterprises. Known for its extremely liberal and inclusive culture, and its liberal environment and penchant for political correctness, Massachusetts was a logical place for Islamic jihad to flourish.

The Boston Islamic Society

The Boston story begins with a small, colorful building on a quiet residential street in Cambridge, Massachusetts, known as the Islamic Society of Boston (ISB). The ISB has been at the center of years of speculation because of the connection of many of its leaders and worshippers to Islamic terrorism. Since its inception, the mosque has

---

[139] "All Dulles Area Muslim Society Center" by Ryan Mauro. Clarion Project, February 5, 2013.

[140] "US Trails Va. Muslim Money, Ties" by Douglas Farrah and John Mintz. October 7, 2002. (No link.)

[141] "Saar Foundation (Safa Trust Group)",
http://www.discoverthenetworks.org/printgroupProfile.asp?grpid=6397

successfully utilized the "media savvy Islamist networks that practice interfaith dialogue in front of the cameras, but preach hatred behind closed doors."[142]

The mosque was founded in 1981, by Abdurahman Alamoudi. Born in Eritrea, Alamoudi immigrated to the U.S. in 1979 and settled in the Boston area, where he soon became active in the local Muslim community. He was active in establishing the ISB, and after signing the Society's articles of incorporation, he served as the mosque's first president until he left Boston for Washington, DC in 1985.[143]

While still in Boston, Alamoudi was allied with the Muslim Brotherhood's spiritual adviser Yousef al-Qaradawi, a terrorist supporter and rabid anti-Semite, who has authored *fatwas* calling for jihad against Israel and the Jews, and authorized suicide-bombing attacks against women

Yousef al-Qaradawi
Photo by Fayex Nuraldine/AFP

---

[142] "From Baghdad to Boston: The moderate Muslims need to be given a prominent space to counter the extremist narrative" by Sam Westrop. *The Nation*, June 15, 2016.
http://nation.com.pk/blogs/15-Jun-2016/from-baghdad-to-boston-the-moderate-muslims-need-to-be-given-a-prominent-space-to-counter-the

[143] Once in Washington, Alamoudi quickly rose to a position of prominence, bringing him close to politicians and presidents. In 2004, however, he fell abruptly from grace when he was convicted for his role in a Libya-sponsored terrorist plan, and sentenced to 23 years in federal prison.

and children.[144] Qaradawi once described the tactic of suicide terrorism against Israeli civilians as "one of the greatest forms of jihad."[145]

Alamoudi was one of the original members of the mosque's Board of Trustees, although his name was suddenly removed from the list following its discovery in 2000.[146] He also served as an "additional trustee" of the Islamic Society of Boston Trust.[147] Although al-Qaradawi was banned from entering the United States in 1999, his name continued to appear on the ISB documents and its website as a trustee for another two years.[148] Despite repeated denials by ISB leaders, al-Qaradawi played a significant role in the creation and development of the mosque, lending it the gravitas associated with his name in the wider Muslim community.

The ISB was the site of many controversial speakers, including Yasir Qadi, who addressed a meeting of the Islamic Society of Boston at its Cambridge mosque. A Muslim employee of the Boston Redevelopment Authority later said about that meeting:

> *"We also are very troubled by a recent sermon given by a visiting preacher, Sheikh Yasir Qadi, at the ISB's Cambridge center. Sheikh Yasir Qadi has previously denied the Holocaust, claimed that Jews want to destroy Muslims, and called all non-Muslims (including Jews and Christians) a "spiritually filthy substance" whose lives and property hold no value and are forfeit to Muslims during Jihad."[149]*

Qadi was well-known for these opinions, which he generally expressed only to Arabic-speaking audiences. An apparently fervent practitioner of

---

[144] Year later, in the early days of the so-called 'Arab Spring' uprising in 2011 and 2012 in Egypt, al-Qaradawi appeared prominently in Cairo's Tahrir Square and addressed a massive demonstration in support the Egyptian Muslim Brotherhood and Mohammed Morsi, who sat beside him on the stage, and would soon begin a short-lived term as the new President of Egypt.

[145] "The Brotherhood must not be seen as moderates" by Hassan Hassan and Ola Salem The National (AE), February 12, 2017. http://www.thenational.ae/opinion/comment/the-brotherhood-must-not-be-seen-as-moderates

[146] Islamic Society of Boston, Form 990, Internal Revenue Service, 2000: http://www.peaceandtolerance.org/wp-content/uploads/sites/4/2016/05/ ISB-990-2000.pdf

[147] Declaration of Trust, Islamic Society of Boston Trust, Middlesex Registry of Deeds, 30 November 1993, http://www.peaceandtolerance.org/wp-content/uploads/sites/4/2015/09/Qaradawi-ISB-trust-land-records-1993.pdf

[148] The Case Against the Islamic Society of Boston, by Americans for Peace and Tolerance. http://www.peaceandtolerance.org/wp-content/uploads/sites/4/2016/05/v2-FINAL-June-2016.pdf

[149] "Muslim Chaplain At Harvard Tells Other Muslims That Yasir Qadi An Authority To Consult [on Taha Abdul-Basser]" *The Iconoclast - New English Review* January 7, 2010 http://www.newenglishreview.org/blog_display.cfm/blog_id/25151h

taqiyya, he refrained from sharing his distasteful views with English-speaking audiences.

In recent years, a growing number of mosques began to appear throughout eastern Massachusetts. Taking advantage of Boston's love for diversity, they were often built in neighborhoods distinguished by their ethnic makeup. These included Sharon, a residential community 30 miles south of Boston, where the Jewish population exceeded 50% of the residents, and the Yusuf Mosque on Beacon Street, where an old American Legion Post was converted into a mosque in the middle of an orthodox Jewish neighborhood of Russian immigrants in the Allston-Brighton area of Boston. Among the most controversial mosques was the Islamic Society of Boston Cultural Center, proposed in 2003, to be built on Malcolm X Boulevard, a largely African-American neighborhood in Roxbury, where a vulnerable population could be targeted for conversions to Islam.

Boston's New Mosque Controversy

A very public controversy erupted when the ISB-sponsored construction of the Islamic Society of Boston Cultural Center (ISBCC) was revealed. The project to build a massive new mosque in the Boston suburb of Roxbury set off a firestorm that involved the Boston Herald, the David Project, and the Mayor of Boston himself. The mosque was to be built on city-owned land that was sold to the ISB for a fraction of its value. The property, valued at $400,000 by the Boston Redevelopment Authority, was sold to the ISB for $175,000[150] in a secret sweetheart deal, arranged by a Muslim employee of the Boston Redevelopment Authority, and approved by Boston's popular mayor, Thomas Menino.

---

[150] "Treasury Department Tars Alamoudi, Founder of the Islamic Society of Boston" December 8, 2005. http://www.defenddemocracy.org/media-hit/treasury-department-tars-alamoudi-founder-of-the-islamic-society-of-boston/#sthash.vjhoeV7N.dpuf

Islamic Society of Boston Cultural Center

A Roxbury resident, James C. Policastro, filed a lawsuit in Suffolk Superior Court against the city of Boston for having subsidized the $22 million Islamic Center.[151] He was backed by the local David Project[152] headed by Charles Jacobs, to stop the project. The lawsuit attracted extensive publicity and media coverage. In 2004, a libel suit was filed by the mosque against the *Boston Herald*, WFXT, the David Project, and others. In the end, the suit was dropped without resolution when the process reached the discovery stage and the ISB declined to proceed. In the end, the mosque was built, but the controversy and the accusations against principals associated with the mosque continued.

The ISB: A Magnet for Terrorists

The ISB in Cambridge is widely thought to have attracted a number of jihadis to its community. including some of the most notorious terrorists complicit in attacks against America.

Abdurahman Alamoudi was one of the most influential terrorist supporters and a participant in many of the organizations described in this monograph. After beginning his American journey in Boston, he moved to the Washington, DC area where, from 1985 to 1990, he served as executive

---

[151] "The Islamic Society of Boston & the Politicians' Red Faces" by Daniel Pipes. Oct 29, 2003. http://www.danielpipes.org/blog/2003/10/the-islamic-society-of-boston- with reference to http://news.bostonherald.com/localRegional/view.bg?articleid=46531

[152] The David Project is a not-for profit organization located in Boston, Massachusetts, whose stated aim is "to positively shape campus opinion on Israel by educating, training, and empowering student leaders to be thoughtful, strategic and persuasive advocates" through relational advocacy

assistant to the president of the SAAR Foundation in northern Virginia. In time, he became the darling of the Washington elite in politics, and was an adviser to Presidents Clinton and Bush alike on matters pertaining to Islam, as well as a frequent guest at the White House and Congress. In 2004, he pleaded guilty to conspiracy charges and received a 23-year sentence in federal prison.

Aafia Siddiqi, a Pakistani neuroscientist, occasionally attended the ISB when she was living in Boston. As a student at MIT in Cambridge, Massachusetts, she was married for a short time to the nephew of al-Qaeda's 9/11 mastermind Khalid Sheik Mohammed. Although she was accused of being involved with 9/11[153], she was arrested in by Afghan police on July 17, 2008 outside the governor's compound in the city of Ghazni, Afghanistan.

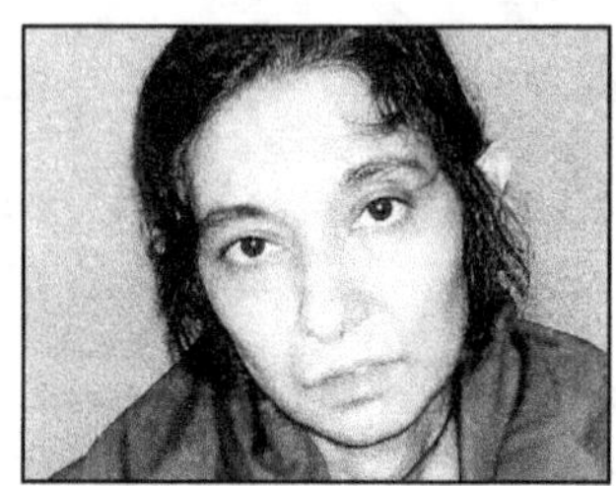

Aafia Siddiqi

She was carrying a handbag containing sodium cyanide in Nivea jars, documents referring to "the creation of explosives and chemical weapons with handwritten instructions for a "dirty bomb," descriptions of key American landmarks, documents about US military assets, and excerpts from "The Anarchist Arsenal."[154]

Siddiqi was turned over to American officials.[155] While under interrogation, Siddiqui grabbed an officer's M4 rifle and began firing. A witness claimed she shouted, "I'm going to kill all you motherfuckers!" and "Death to America." She was shot twice, and in September 2008, she was indicted. Following her trial in 2010, Siddiqui was sentenced to 86 years in prison for planning a chemical attack on New York City and for the attempted murder of two U.S soldiers.[156]

In August 2014, the Islamic State (IS) reportedly tried unsuccessfully to trade her release for IS hostages, journalists James Foley and Steven Sotloff. Both were later beheaded in widely-circulated videos.[157]

Tamerlan and Dzhokhar Tsarnaev, two brothers who perpetrated the Boston Marathon Bombing on April 13, 2013, both attended the ISB. The leaders of the Islamic Society mosque claimed that Tamerlan's ideology

---

[153] In March 2003, she was named as a courier and financier for Al-Qaeda by Khalid Sheikh Muhammad and was placed on a "wanted for questioning" list by the American FBI.

[154] "Who's Afraid of Aafia Siddiqui?" by Katherine Ozment. Boston Magazine, October 2004. http://www.bostonmagazine.com/2006/05/whos-afraid-of-aafia-siddiqui/

[155] "Aafia Siddiqui: The Woman Isis Wanted To Trade For Foley, Then Sotloff" by Janine di Giovanni. Newsweek, 16, 2014. http://www.newsweek.com/2014/09/26/aafia-siddiqui-woman-isis-wanted-trade-foley-then-sotloff-270830.html

[156] Ibid

[157] Ibid

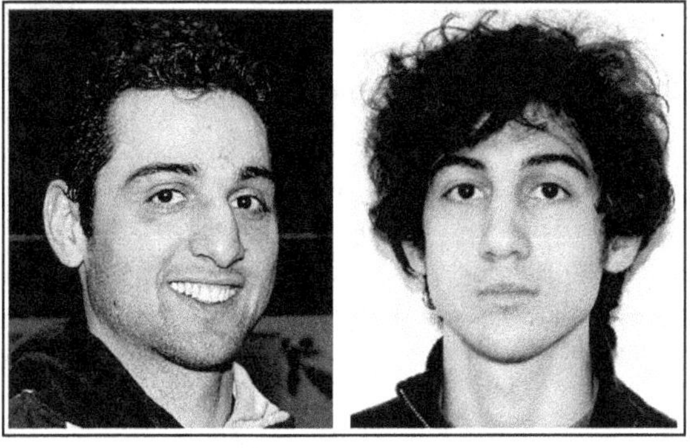

Tamerlan and Dzhokhar Tsarnaev

was more 'extreme' than theirs. In fact, they said, he was chastised for an 'extremist' outburst he made during one sermon.[158] Although the FBI was warned by the Russians multiple times after his 2012 trip to Russia, U.S. officials did not pursue the matter. Tamerlan was also implicated in the brutal murder of three men in Waltham, Massachusetts in September 2011, but had not been apprehended before the marathon bombing.[159] On April 8, 2015, Dzhokhar Tsarnaev, the surviving brother, was convicted of using a weapon of mass destruction resulting in the death of three people and injury of at least 264 others, and was sentenced to death a month later.

Osama M. Kandil was one of the leaders of the Islamic Society of Boston for more than ten years. A former instructor at Harvard Medical School and founder and chairman of Biopharm Group, an Egyptian pharmaceutical company, Kandil was associated with the Safa Group and was a founding director of the Muslim Arab Youth Association, one of the radical Islamist youth organizations in the United States operating under the aegis of the Muslim Brotherhood. In the list of Safa Group companies compiled by Safa Group Businesses & Corporations (as recorded by NEFA Foundation and the Investigative Project), Kandil is also listed as an agent for American Products International, Inc., one of the Safa Group front companies.[160]

Walid Ahmad Fitaihi was a trustee and a member of the Islamic Society of Boston's board of directors.[161] He is a American Board Certified

---

[158] "Boston bombers' mosque tied to ISIS" by Paul Sperry. New York Post, September 7, 2014. http://nypost.com/2014/09/07/jihadi-behind-beheading-videos-linked-to-notorious-us-mosque/

[159] "Tsarnaev allegedly knew brother was part of triple slaying" by Derek J. Anderson. Boston Globe, October 12, 2011. https://www.bostonglobe.com/metro/2014/10/11/witness-can-testify-that-bombing-suspect-tsarnaev-knew-brother-was-involved-waltham-triple-slaying-according-court-filing/dEFhb6pk9HrNC8XOXWMbYM/story.html

[160] "Terror Tied Islamic Society Of Boston And Islamist Imam Suhaib Webb Play Victims And Ask Police For Protection" Militant Islam Monitor, April 17, 2013. http://www.militantislammonitor.org/article/id/5739

[161] "The Islamic Society of Boston & the Politicians' Red Faces" by Daniel Pipes, October 29, 2003. http://www.danielpipes.org/blog/2003/10/the-islamic-society-of-boston-the

physician specializing in endocrinology. He and his father gave $2,387,025 to the ISB. Among his antisemitic writings, the London-based, Arabic language "Al-Sharq al Awsat" published the following libel about the Jews, written by Fitaihi, on October 18, 2000: [162]

> *"[S]courged [because of their] oppression, murder, and rape of the worshippers of Allah...They have perpetrated the worst of evils and they have brought the worst corruption to the earth, and what we see of them these days is glad tidings for the Muslim heralding the fulfillment of Allah's promise of victory after the second transgression."*

His sentiments were made public in 2003, but he responded by saying he was mistranslated. In October 2004, however, the Boston Globe published a letter by Ahmed H. al-Rahim, an instructor of Arabic language

Dr. Walid Ahmad Fitaihi

and literature at Harvard University and chairman of the American Islamic Congress, in which he wrote:

"I read the writings of Dr. Walid Fitaihi in both the Arabic and the English translations, and found them to be virulently antisemitic. It is not a question of "errors in translation from Arabic to English" as Dr. Fitaihi claims. The anti-Semitism exhibited in his writings is the same whether it is in Arabic or English. Dr. Fitaihi's current role in the Islamic Society of Boston raises more questions than it answers, questions that the society needs to answer directly and unequivocally."[163]

In 2000, the Boston Herald reported that a London-based newspaper had quoted Fitaihi calling Jews the "murderers of prophets." According to the article, Fitaihi predicted that they would be cursed because of their "oppression, murder and rape of the worshippers of Allah." Violence against Israelis was a "great thing, he said."[164] Despite these clearly antisemitic statements, Fitaihi retained his position as Trustee of the ISB. In fact,

---

[162] "Bank Records Reveal Saudi Elites Gave Millions to Boston Marathon Bombers' Mosque" Counter Jihad Report. https://counterjihadreport.com/tag/walid-fitaihi/

[163] "The Islamic Society of Boston & the Politicians' Red Faces" by Daniel Pipes, October 29, 2003. http://www.danielpipes.org/blog/2003/10/the-islamic-society-of-boston-the

[164] "City will look closer at mosque terror link" by Tom Mashberg. *Boston Herald*, Thursday, October 7, 2004
https://web.archive.org/web/20041012223732/http://news.bostonherald.com/localRegiona
l/view.bg?articleid=47880

mosque posted on its Web site a response to criticism of his statements, saying that "the articles were intended to condemn particular individuals ... not meant to incite hatred of an entire faith or people."[165] The ISB denied any connection to radical Islam (a claim easily made, as faithful adherence to Islamic doctrine is hardly considered 'radical' among devout Muslims.)

Jamal Badawi, another former trustee, Islamic cleric and lecturer at the ISB. He was IAU vice-chairman, past or current board member of FCNA, ISNA, CAIR, CCNA, the European Council of Fatwa and Research (ECFR), and the International Union of Islamic Scholars (IUIS). He was named as an unindicted co-conspirator in the Holy Land Foundation trial.

Tarek Mehanna was a frequent worshipper at the ISB. He was convicted and sentenced for his travels to Yemen with Ahmad Abousamra (see below) in 2004, in search, the government said, of a jihadi training camp from which they would then proceed to Iraq to fight American nationals.[166] After Mehanna returned home, he "continued his efforts to provide material support by, among other things, translating and posting on the Internet al Qaeda recruitment videos and other documents." He was arrested in 2008 for making "false statements to the FBI." In 2009, he was

Tarek Mehanna

indicted for providing "material support for terrorism" by advocating jihad from his home in Sudbury. In April 2012, he was sentenced to 17 years in federal prison. He was also accused of conspiring with Abousamra to shoot random shoppers in a suburban mall near Boston, then fire on the emergency responders.[167]

Ahmad Abousamra, a dual US-Syrian citizen who was born in France but grew up in Stoughton, Massachusetts, also worshipped at the Cambridge mosque, and was reportedly inspired by the 9/11 attacks. Abousamra was indicted in 2009 for conspiracy to provide material support

---

[165] "Treasury Department Tars Alamoudi, Founder of the Islamic Society of Boston" December 8, 2005 http://www.defenddemocracy.org/media-hit/treasury-department-tars-alamoudi-founder-of-the-islamic-society-of-boston/#sthash.vjhoeV7N.dpuf

[166] "Tarek Mehanna Sentenced in Boston to 17 Years in Prison on Terrorism-Related Charges", S Attorney's Office, District of Massachusetts. April 12, 2012.
https://archives.fbi.gov/archives/boston/press-releases/2012/tarek-mehanna-sentenced-in-boston-to-17-years-in-prison-on-terrorism-related-charges

[167] Ibid

Abousamra before and after joining IS
(Photo: FBI file)

to terrorists; providing and attempting to provide material support to terrorists; conspiracy to kill in a foreign country; conspiring to support al-Qaeda; and false statements, and indicted by a federal grand jury.[168] He was added to the FBI's Most Wanted list in 2013, under a $50,000 bounty.[169] After traveling to Syria and joining the Islamist State, he became its top propagandist. Operating under the nickname Abu Samra, he was one of the masterminds behind its sophisticated and highly effective media campaign that included the extensive distribution of beheadings and other savage atrocities through gruesome videos that they posted on the Internet. His campaign helped recruit at least 300 Americans, as well as thousands of other English speaking, would-be jihadis from around the world. He was reported by multiple sources to have been killed in an Iraqi airstrike in May 2016.

Others associated with Islamic terrorism who attended the Boston mosque are:

Yasir al-Qadi, who lectured at ISB's Boston mosque in 2009 and again in 2012, advocates replacing American democracy with shariah; characterizes Christians as "filthy" polytheists whose "life and prosperity ... holds no value in the state of Jihad"; and accuses Jews of plotting to destroy Muslim peoples and societies. Qadi is an acolyte of Ali

Yasir Qadi

al-Timimi, a Virginia-based Imam, who is currently serving life in prison for inciting jihad against U.S. troops in Afghanistan.

Al-Qadi once described the "eternal conflict between Muslims and non-Muslims" in the following manner:

"And this is the Sunnah [Practice] of Allah that the Kafir [disbeliever] will always hate the Muslim - the Jews and the

---

[168] FBI Most Wanted. https://www.fbi.gov/wanted/wanted_terrorists/ahmad-abousamra/@@download.pdf

[169] "Mass. man accused of aiding ISIS killed in Iraq, reports say" Boston Globe, June 3, 2015. https://www.bostonglobe.com/metro/2015/06/03/mass-man-accused-aiding-isis-killed-iraq-reports-say/MABevJO6Pm4beu1B8M1yHI/story.html

*Christians and the Hindus and every single non-Muslim," he said
in an undated sermon. "He might allow every other religious
minority or any other religion inside of his society and culture,
but when it comes to Islam, because it is the religion of truth, he
will find it inside of him to hate it. You cannot just be neutral when it
comes to Islam; you are either a Muslim or you are a Kaffir that hates
Islam."*[170]

Supporting Terrorists

Islamic Society leaders have been consistently supportive of their
worshippers who have been accused or convicted of terrorism and have
openly defended them. They have attended their hearings and trials,
lobbied for their release or have demanded more lenient sentences. They
have held fundraisers and rallies for the terrorists,[171] hosted pro-jihad
speakers, and stocked their library with classic jihadi texts, including the
writings Syed Qutb, the inspiration for the modern jihadi revival in Islam.[172]

Again and again, the Islamic Center of Boston has been connected to
terrorists and their supporters who have come, however briefly, as
members of their congregation, as leaders of the community, as members of
its Board of Directors, or as trustees. The Islamic Society of Boston has a
long record of welcoming people who then commit heinous acts of terror.
Supported by CAIR, and by individuals associated with a variety of Muslim
Brotherhood organizations, one might ask, "How many of these cases need
to happen before it stops being a coincidence"?

Hamas Goes to Work: The Ptech Story

Among the most chilling of the plots that thrive in the deep web of
organizations created by the Muslim Brotherhood are those that not only
involve using legitimate companies to hide the Brotherhood's money-
laundering support for Hamas, but also pose a significant threat to
America's national security. Here again, the Boston area seems to be a hub
for such terror-connected activity.

The Ptech case involved a small hi-tech company in Quincy,
Massachusetts, which produced and marketed a package of enterprise
software to federal government agencies and major corporations. Ptech

---

[170] "ICNA Embraces America's Favorite Salafi Preacher" *IPT News* August 1, 2012
http://www.investigativeproject.org/3692/icna-embraces-america-favorite-salafi-preacher#

[171] "Mass. man accused of aiding ISIS killed in Iraq, reports say" Boston Globe, June 3, 2015.
https://www.bostonglobe.com/metro/2015/06/03/mass-man-accused-aiding-isis-killed-
iraq-reports-say/MABevJO6Pm4beu1B8M1yHI/story.html

[172] Qutb was a senior theoretician of the Muslim Brotherhood whose writing galvanized
devout Muslims around the world to jihad. His seminal *Milestones* monograph has been found
on the person of jihadis on battlefields all over the world.

was a rising star, and considered one of the fastest growing hi-tech companies in New England. It was a global supplier of software designed to help its clients visualize and analyze its technical infrastructure and build models for business planning that would enable management to make informed choices.

In an article distributed by the Associated Press in 2003, Justin Pope wrote that Ptech's software "visually represents large amounts of information . . . to help complicated organizations like the military and large companies create a picture of how their assets -- people and technology -- work together. Then the software could show how little changes, like combining two departments, might affect the whole."[173]

According to the website at the time (no longer on-line), Ptech's client list was comprised of powerful, high profile clients. Its story is important because its enterprise software was installed on government computers throughout the country, including the Department of Justice, the Department of Energy, Treasury Department, CIA, FBI, Air Force, Navy, Department of Energy, IRS, U.S. Customs, the FAA, and even the White House. Corporate clients included IBM, Aetna, Motorola, Enron (now defunct), and many more.

Ptech had a good beginning. It was founded in 1994 by Oussama Ziade, Hussein Ibrahim, and James Cerrato, with a $20 million start-up investment from BMI, Inc. (Bait ul-Mal or House of Wealth), a real estate investment firm in Secaucus, New Jersey. The company claimed to have over $1 million under management, as well as housing developments in Maryland and Indiana. Its projected revenues were said to be in excess of $25 million.[174]

But at least one of its funders (and, as it turned out, the funding company itself), as well as several of its founders and employees, had ties to terrorist organizations. What is crucial to the story is that the software systems were embedded throughout critically sensitive federal agencies and global corporations. It is not difficult to imagine the possible security issues in this scenario. And even though the White House assured America that no "classified products" were found in the software, the question remained as to whether the software itself could contain a threat because it was designed "to develop enterprise blueprints that held every important functional, operational, and technical detail of a given enterprise."[175] Such data in the wrong hands might certainly pose a threat to the government and to the highest levels of national security.

---

[173] "Software company tries to survive terrorism investigation", by Justin Pope, Associated Press, January 3, 2003. http://www.boston.com/news/daily/03/ptech.htm

[174] Statement of Richard A. Clarke Before the United States Senate Banking Committee. October 22, 2003. http://www.investigativeproject.org/documents/testimony/54.pdf

[175] "The Business of Terror", FrontPageMagazine.com, by Dr. Rachel Ehrenfeld. June 17, 2005. http://archive.frontpagemag.com/bioAuthor.aspx?AUTHID=359

While posing as a legitimate company, BMI was, in fact, a Hamas front, whose investor list read like a who's who of designated terrorists. The money trail leading back to the original funders and principals in the company was revealing because it included some of the leading names in the Hamas/CAIR/Muslim Brotherhood nexus. Among them were:

Soliman Biheiri was the head of BMI. U.S. prosecutors later called him "the United States banker for the Muslim Brotherhood" and "the Muslim Brotherhood's toehold in the United States."[176] His ties to al-Taqwa Bank,[177] the largest financial supporter of al-Qaeda and Hamas, included financial transactions and contact information for terrorist financiers. Biheiri was convicted of illegal financial dealings with Marzook, who had already been labeled a designated terrorist, and accused of lying to a federal agent and immigration fraud.[178]

Yasin al-Qadi was a Saudi multi-millionaire, whose company, Kadi International, operated from the same office as BMI. Al-Qadi invested $5 million in Ptech through the company Sarmani Ltd,[179] and had financial dealings with Yaqub Mirza, who was deeply involved with the Safa network in Virginia. Shortly after 9/11, al-Qadi was considered a suspected terrorist financier.

Mousa Abu Marzook and **Abdurahman Alamoudi** were among the 50 or so investors who contributed to Ptech.

In addition to the participation of known Hamas operatives, investigative journalist Michael Kane summarized the allegations:

> *"Among the financiers and programmers of Ptech are apparent members of an international network of organized criminals involved in decades of narcotraffic, gunrunning, money laundering, and terrorism. Their personal and professional connections reach up into the highest levels of the American government, and their activities are still underway."*[180]

In October 2001, the FBI received warnings from Ptech employees that Yasin al-Qadi had been one of the funders of Ptech. Indira Singh, who was at the time an employee at JP Morgan Chase bank, was assigned by the bank to investigate Ptech, preliminary to a potential business deal. By May 2002,

---

[176] HR 3892 – Bill to Designate Muslim Brotherhood a foreign terrorist organization. November 3, 2015. www.congress.gov/114/hr3892/BILLS-114hr3892ih.pdf

[177] The US Treasury Department reported that in 1997 alone, more than $60 million passed through al-Taqwa Bank on its way to Hamas.

[178] http://www.historycommons.org/entity.jsp?entity=oussama_ziade

[179] "Ptech Inc.", History Commons, http://www.historycommons.org/entity.jsp?entity=ptech_inc

[180] "PTECH, 9/11, and USA-SAUDI TERROR - Part II", by Michael Kane, From The Wilderness, 2005, http://www.fromthewilderness.com/free/ww3/012705_ptech_pt2.shtml

her suspicions about Ptech were serious enough for her to bring her concerns to the FBI. Singh, whose specialty was "risk architecture, later wrote:

"I invited Ptech to come down and give a presentation and a customized demo to JP Morgan Chase." At the time, she was designing a system for JP Morgan Chase to detect terrorist money laundering.[181] ... Within half an hour on the premises, I knew something was up. They had almost immediately raised about six of my red flags, to the point where I walked over to my desk and picked up the phone, and began making phone calls."

Al-Qadi's deep involvement a Virginia-based group of Muslim charities and businesses with documented, direct connections to terror-financing fronts and terror groups directly.

> *The alleged terrorist at issue is Yassin Qadi, who invested more than $10.3 million in Ptech and obtained more than a third of the company's stock in return. Qadi was designated by the U.S. Treasury Department in October 2001 for alleged ties to Al Qaeda, a move that was supposed to freeze his assets.*
>
> *Ziade was aware of the order, the indictment said, but did nothing to block Qadi's assets. Rather, he arranged a series of transactions designed to hide them. When federal agents questioned Ziade in December 2002, he claimed he didn't know the amount of Qadi's ownership interest in Ptech.*
>
> *The indictment cites a 1997 letter in which Ziade called Qadi "the major shareholder as well as a key member of the board" of Ptech.[182]*

After several months, upon learning that the FBI was not moving forward with the investigation, Singh contacted reporter Joe Bergantino at Boston's WBZ television station, who began his own investigation of Ptech. In late August 2002, the federal government also opened an investigation into terrorist financing, which it called "Operation Green Quest." According to the Associated Press,[183] US agents called Ptech management directly and asked them about their ties to money laundering. WBZ-TV prepared a story on Ptech, but did not air it for more than three months, after receiving

---

[181] "Ptech/CVE.MITRE.ORG/DHS/Horizons/EA/IT Governance/USAID" PrisonPlanet http://forum.prisonplanet.com/index.php?topic=80222.0

[182] Ptech Officials Indicted for Allegedly Concealing Terror Financier's Assets, IPT News July 16, 2009. https://www.investigativeproject.org/1094/ptech-officials-indicted-for-allegedly-concealing

[183] "Software company tries to survive terrorism investigation", by Justin Pope, Associated Press, January 3, 2003. http://www.boston.com/news/daily/03/ptech.htm

requests to suppress it in the form of "calls from federal law enforcement agencies, some at the highest levels."[184]

On the evening of December 6, 2002, during a heavy snowstorm, Ptech was raided by a multi-agency team that included the IRS, U.S. Customs, and, to a lesser extent, the FBI and others. The raid was based on a tip from an employee, who told them he suspected the company was connected to 9/11.[185]

It was not the usual kind of federal agency raid, however, because the element of surprise was completely lacking. Company officers had been warned a month earlier that they were being investigated and, soon before the raid, they were informed when it would take place. After waiting for more than five hours in the Ptech parking lot, the agents received orders to begin the raid and they descended upon the office. What they found was that Ptech operated with a largely paperless system, so rather than removing boxes of files as they had in Virginia, they removed computers and associated electronic equipment.

Only hours after the raid on Ptech, the White House issued a statement, through its press secretary Ari Fleisher, saying, "The one thing I can share with you is that the products that were supplied by this company to the government all fell in the non-classified area. None of it involved any classified products used by the government. The material has been reviewed by the appropriate government agencies, and they have detected absolutely nothing in their reports to the White House that would lead to any concern about any of the products purchased from this company."[186] By May 2004, no charges had been filed, and no arrests were made.

Not surprisingly, although the search into Ptech was a part of the ongoing 'Operation Green Quest,[187] the Ptech investigation went nowhere.[188] The purpose of Operation Green Quest was "to augment existing counter-terrorist efforts by bringing the full scope of the government's financial expertise to bear against systems, individuals, and

---

[184] "Channel 4, First on the Story, Abided by US Reaquest Not to Air It" by Mark Jurkowitz. Boston Globe, January 7, 2007. (Link expired)

[185] "The Business of Terrorism" by Rachel Ehrenfeld.
http://archive.frontpagemag.com/readArticle.aspx?ARTID=8245

[186] Press Briefing by White House Spokesman Ari Fleisher. The White House, December 6, 2002.

[187] Operation Green Quest was federal interagency investigation initiated in October 2001 after 9/11. It was led by the United States Customs Service and was focused on the surveillance and interdiction of terrorist financing. It was disbanded in June 2003 following an agreement between the Department of Homeland Security and the Department of Justice.

[188] Ibid.

organizations that serve as sources of terrorist funding."[189] Over a period of 14 months, Operation Green Quest served 114 search warrants involving suspected terrorist financing that resulted in fifty arrests in which $27.4 million seized,[190] but although Ptech had clear connections to Hamas-related financing, the federal government dismissed any Hamas connection to the company.

After the so-called investigation, Ptech changed its name to GoAgile, and although it lost some of its clients because of the unfavorable publicity it received following the raid, Boston's Patriot Ledger quoted CEO Oussama Ziade, "We still have government agencies as customers, including the White House."[191]

In short, the company continued operations despite its clear links to terrorism. What seems to have been lost in the investigations, which searched for connections among Ptech, Saudi Arabia, and 9/11, were the clear associations between Ptech and principals actively engaged in money laundering for Hamas.

The government's refusal to pursue the investigation did not make the concerns go away. Conspiracy theories abounded regarding Ptech's connection to everything terrorism. The facts, however, are clear when it comes to the money trail. They all led back to Hamas.

In a letter dated January 22, 2003, Chuck Grassley, senior U.S. Senator from Iowa, wrote to FBI Director Robert Muller: "I am concerned…[with] vulnerabilities which might arise from using Ptech software."[192] He was right to be concerned. If, as the evidence suggests, Ptech was affiliated, directly or indirectly, with Hamas, then the vulnerability that it presented to national security was, as Senator Grassley ,suggested, considerably more than just a serious concern.

Despite the government's reluctance to link Ptech with Hamas in 2003, Ptech's CEO Oussama Ziade was indicted by the FBI six years later on charges of dealing in the property of Yasin al-Qadi, a Specially Designated Global Terrorist, failing to block the terrorist's assets, and making false statements to federal investigators.[193] Ptech's former COO Buford George Peterson was also indicted for making false statements on a Small Business Administration loan application to hide the fact that a Specially Designated

---

[189] U.S. Customs Service Launches "operation Green Quest": Multi-Agency Initiative to Target Sources of Funding for Terrorist Organizations The Avalon Project, Yale Law School. http://avalon.law.yale.edu/sept11/customs_002.asp

[190] "Feds Look for Data on Saudi in Ptech Raid" by Arik Hesseldahl. *Forbes* December 6, 2002. (link expired)

[191] Patriot Ledger, May 14, 2004. (link no longer available)

[192] Ibid

[193] "Former Ptech Officer Arrested for SBA Loan Fraud" U.S. Attorney's Office, July 15, 2009. www.archives.fbi.gov/archives/boston/press-releases/2009/bs071509.htm

Global Terrorist held a $10 million stake in Ptech. Peterson, who had been living in South Korea, was arrested when he returned to the U.S. as he was getting of the plane at New York's JFK airport.[194] At the time of the publication of this book, Oussama Ziade is still a fugitive.[195]

Although Yaqub Mirza represented Yasin al-Qadi and managed foundations whose principals were accused of funding terrorist group, he has never been charged with a crime. Earlier on, he served as CEO of Sterling Advisory Services, which controlled many of the 555 Grove Street entities. Sterling Advisory Services also controlled "Ptech Fund LLC" and Mirza sat on the board of Ptech. Today he is President and CEO of the Sterling Management Group, with offices in Herndon, Virginia.

---

[194] "Ptech Officials Indicted for Allegedly Concealing Terror Financier's Assets", *IPT News* July 16, 2009. http://www.investigativeproject.org/1094/ptech-officials-indicted-for-allegedly-concealing

[195] "Former Ptech Officer Arrested for SBA Loan Fraud," Federal Bureau of Investigation, 15 July 2009, accessed 5/20/16: https://www.fbi.gov/ boston/press-releases/2009/bs071509.htm

Hamas Goes To College

For decades, American college campuses have been prime targets for Arab activists in their anti-Israel obsession. On campuses around the country, they give vocal and often violent expression to their claims on Israeli territory and of realizing their dream of "driving the Jews into the sea." [196] Once established in the U.S., Hamas initiated a campaign of recruitment through a growing network of Muslim groups, including student groups spawned by the Muslim Brotherhood such as MAYA and MSA. As a result of these efforts, Hamas supporters began to appear in growing numbers on college campuses throughout America, attracting progressive and disaffected students to activism, making news and influencing school policy.

Today, Hamas' influence at colleges and universities across the country is open and loud. Acts of anti-Israel activism as well as open and virulent anti-Semitism have skyrocketed on campuses across the United States. Pro-Palestinian groups sponsor anti-Israel events, disrupt Israeli and pro-Israel speakers with raucous heckling, sometimes barring entrance to would-be attendees, and even forcing the cancellation of pro-Israel events with threats of violence. Their view of First Amendment rights applies only to themselves and others who share their political views. Those who disagree or do not share their point of view are not granted the same freedom of speech.

Prominent among the groups sponsoring these disruptive and divisive activities are American Muslims for Palestine (AMP) and Boycott, Divestment, and Sanctions (BDS), both funded, directly or indirectly, by Hamas, as well as by left-wing, progressive groups like change.org, George Soros's Open Society Foundation, and the New Israel Fund.[197]

---

[196] "Islamic Jerusalem: 'We Will Drive the Jews into the Sea'" MuslimMatters.org http://muslimmatters.org/2009/07/29/islamic-jerusalem-"we-will-drive-the-jews-into-the-sea"-3-of-3/

[197] "Not Shocking: George Soros Funds Progressive War on Israel" by Abraham H. Miller. *The Observer,* August 17, 2016 http://observer.com/2016/08/not-shocking-george-soros-funds-progressive-war-on-israel/10

Anti-Israel demonstration at University of California
where demonstrators shouted, "We are Hamas."

In recent years, there has been a "surge in the number of invited campus speakers being repeatedly interrupted or actually prevented from delivering a public lecture. A startling share of these silencing efforts has been directed at Israelis or other speakers sympathetic to Israel who have run afoul of the growing anti-Israel movement on campuses."[198]

These actions are not grounded in frustrations over a failed 'peace process' between Israel and the Palestinians. The reality is quite the opposite. Cary Nelson and David Greenberg explained it this way:

"Behind this spike is an idea called "anti-normalization." This concept, which anti-Israel organizations began vigorously promoting two years ago, holds that any activities that might "normalize" relations between Israelis and Palestinians — from children's soccer leagues to collaborative environmental projects to university panel discussions with both sides represented — should be summarily rejected because they treat both parties as having legitimate grievances and aspirations. Joint projects are to be shunned unless they begin with the premise that Israel is the guilty party."[199]

---

[198] "Students are shouting down pro-Israel speakers — and silencing free speech" by Cary Nelson and David Greenberg. *Washington Post*, December 7
https://www.washingtonpost.com/opinions/students-are-shouting-down-pro-israel-speakers--and-silencing-free-speech/2016/12/07/9211c3b8-bbd7-11e6-91ee-1adddfe36cbe_story.html?utm_term=.6cb254d79f57

[199] Ibid

San Francisco State Shows Open Support for Hamas

There is no shortage of examples that demonstrate how this policy is carried out. In April 2016, for example, San Francisco State University (SFSU) campus police did nothing to interfere with demonstrators from the General Union of Palestinian Students (GUPS) when they disrupted a speech by Jerusalem Mayor Nir Barkat, who had been invited by San Francisco Hillel, a Jewish student group. So loud was the wild and raucous shouting from the GUPS students that hearing Barkat "proved to be impossible as the incessant threats and amplified chants prevented anyone from hearing Mayor Barkat's speech or engaging in dialog with him. ... With their verbal assaults, angry gestures, and hostile actions, the disrupting students physically threatened Plaintiffs and others in attendance, who feared for their safety," according to a lawsuit filed by The Lawfare Project, a legal group dedicated to fighting anti-Semitism.[200]

Newsweek reported that the lawsuit argues the demonstration against Barkat was only one of a number of incidents that "contributed to an atmosphere hostile to Jewish students, one that was created with the alleged complicity of the school's administrations." filed the lawsuit on behalf of six individuals who attended the event. The lawsuit claims "SFSU allows for mob rule at the expense of civil rights," the suit says, "where the loudest and most aggressive group rules the day."

The demonstrators claimed to be protesting what they called the university's active involvement "in creating safe spaces for hate speech and the promotion of international law violations by offering a stage for Barkat."[201] They received tacit support

SFSU President Leslie Wong

from University President Leslie Wong following the event, when he put out a weak statement to the students, saying only, "Members of our community who attended the event were deprived of an opportunity to hear from the Mayor."[202]

The lawsuit, filed the following year, cited Wong, the trustees of the university, and the larger California State University system (of which SFSU

---

[200] "Middle East Conflict Comes To U.S. Campuses As Jewish Students File Anti-Semitism Suit" by Alexander Nazaryan. Newsweek.com, 6/25/17. http://www.newsweek.com/anti-semitism-alleged-san-fran-state-628469

[201] "Students explain why they protested Jerusalem mayor Nir Barkat at San Francisco State University" by Mondoweiss Editors. Mondoweiss, May 5, 2016 http://mondoweiss.net/2016/05/protested-jerusalem-university/#sthash.wud6akdD.dpuf

[202] Message from President Wong: Civil Discourse" SF State News. Thursday, April 07, 2016 https://news.sfsu.edu/announcements/message-president-wong-civil-discourse

is a member) as defendants. The suit called SFSU "among the worst of the worst offenders and is largely recognized as being among the most antisemitic campuses in the country. ... SFSU allows for mob rule at the expense of civil rights where the loudest and most aggressive group rules the day."[203]

In another flagrant expression of support for Hamas and rejection of the 'peace process', President Wong implemented a Memorandum of Understanding (MOU) with An-Najah University in the West Bank. An-Najah has been described by Hamas as a "greenhouse for martyrs" and the Palestinian university has fomented incitement to violence, antisemitism, and the veneration of terrorism against Israel. An-Najah is widely known for the terrorist recruitment, indoctrination, and radicalization of students that is rampant there. The school is also notorious for its 'Sbarro Cafe Exhibition', a celebration of a suicide bombing attack that took place at the Jerusalem restaurant on August 9, 2001. Fifteen people were murdered, seven of them children, and 130 were wounded and maimed.

The gruesome display, which was put on by student supporters of Hamas, which claimed responsibility for the attack, was replete with broken furniture splattered with fake blood and human body parts. When the exhibit opened, it was said to have attracted thousands of people, most of them university students.[204]

In 2010, six members of the An-Najah faculty were arrested by Palestinian Authority security forces, accused of being closely linked to a charity suspected of being a front for Hamas.[205] In 2013, An-Najah named an entire graduating class after Abu Jihad, the founder of Fatah and the

---

[203] "Middle East Conflict Comes To U.S. Campuses As Jewish Students File Anti-Semitism Suit" by Alexander Nazaryan. Newsweek.com, 6/25/17. http://www.newsweek.com/anti-semitism-alleged-san-fran-state-628469

[204] "Gruesome exhibit marks anniversary of uprising" by The Associated Press, September 24, 2001

[205] "6 Faculty Members at a Palestinian University Are Arrested for Suspected Hamas Ties", by Matthew Kalman. *The Chronicle of Higher Education*, August 04, 2010. http://www.chronicle.com/article/6-Faculty-Members-at-a/123764/

mastermind of many brutal terror attacks. At An-Najah's June 2014 graduation ceremony, students held up three fingers to celebrate Hamas' kidnapping and murder of three Israeli teenagers.[206]

Showing complete indifference to these clear signs of support for a designated terrorist group, Wong signed the MOU with An-Najah. At the time, he said, "When I returned from Palestine two years ago, I said I want to be one of the first major universities to sign an agreement with An-Najah or any of the other Palestinian universities, or any of the universities in the Arab world." The terms of the MOU between the two universities are secret, raising questions of how complicit SFSU's relationship may be regarding An-Najah's open support for Hamas.

More Campus Support for Hamas-led Chaos by Once-Proud Universities

- In September 2011, a group of ten University of California-Irvine students and a representative from American Muslims for Palestine (AMP) were arrested and prosecuted for organizing and carrying out the disruption of a speech on the campus of UC Irvine by Israeli Ambassador Michael Oren. They tried to prevent him from delivering his lecture by heckling and shouting in a manner that Orange County District Attorney Tony Rackauckas called "censorship and 'thuggery'."[207]

- In April 2014, Brandeis University announced that it had withdrawn its invitation to Ayaan Hirsi Ali, who was to have been awarded an honorary degree. The retraction followed what was called a 'grassroots' campaign to withdraw the degree. In fact, it was far more than a 'grassroots' effort. "In an open letter to Brandeis University, CAIR, Ibrahim Hooper used one of its usual ploys to silence critics, attacking Hirsi Ali personally by calling her a "notorious Islamophobe," and "one of the worst of the worst of the Islam haters in America, not only in America but worldwide." He compared honoring her with "promoting the work of a white supremacist."[208]

---

[206] "Research on Terrorism and Extremism at An-Najah University" by Cinnamon Stillwell. Campus Watch, September 15, 2016. http://www.campus-watch.org/article/id/16444

[207] "Students guilty of disrupting speech in 'Irvine 11' case" by Lauren Williams, Nicole Santa Cruz and Mike Anton, *Los Angeles Times*, September 24, 2011. http://articles.latimes.com/2011/sep/24/local/la-me-irvine-eleven-20110924

[208] "Brandeis Cancels Plan to Give Honorary Degree to Ayaan Hirsi Ali, a Critic of Islam" by Richard Pérez-Peña And Tanzina Vega. New York Times, April 8, 2014. https://www.nytimes.com/2014/04/09/us/brandeis-cancels-plan-to-give-honorary-degree-to-ayaan-hirsi-ali-a-critic-of-islam.html?_r=0

Hirsi Ali, born a Muslim in Somalia, was to have been honored for her outspoken fight for women's rights, but, because she is also a strong critic of Islam, an online petition sponsored by change.org labeled her an Islamophobe. The university made a statement about its reversal in which it said, "We cannot overlook certain of her past statements that are inconsistent with Brandeis University's core values. ... For all concerned, we regret that we were not aware of these statements earlier."[209]

The BDS Movement

By far the most vocal, Hamas-driven group on college campuses today is the Boycott, Divest, and Sanctions (BDS) movement, which was launched in 2005. In slightly less than 12 years, BDS has spread rapidly across the country and throughout Europe. From the beginning, its goals have been to delegitimize Israel through economic and academic boycotts, by demonizing Israel's responses to Islamic terror attacks, and by either condemning or denying Israel's commitment to democratic principles.

BDS was an offspring of the "Arab Boycott" movement, founded in December 1945 by the newly formed Arab League Council, three years before the founding of the Jewish state. In its founding declaration, the words "Jewish" and "Zionist" were used interchangeably. It read, in part: "Jewish products and manufactured goods shall be considered undesirable to the Arab countries." Arab owned "institutions, organizations, merchants, commission agents and individuals" were requested "to refuse to deal in, distribute, or consume Zionist products or manufactured goods."[210]

Shortly after its founding sixty years later, BDS claimed the support of over 170 Palestinian organizations. The Palestinian Civil Society conference called for a BDS campaign against Israeli companies operating in the West Bank and the Golan Heights.[211] This initial goal quickly morphed into a boycott of everything Israel (while avoiding the obviously inconvenient divestment of such Israeli inventions as critical components of their personal computers and cell phones, instant messaging, life-saving medical devices, and much more).

Ties between Hamas-linked charities and BDS were highlighted in Congressional testimony by Jonathan Schanzer, which cited research that

---

[209] "Why Brandeis Revoked Its Invitation For Ayaan Hirsi Ali To Receive An Honorary Degree" by Ben Armbruster. *New York Times,* April 11, 2014. https://thinkprogress.org/why-brandeis-revoked-its-invitation-for-ayaan-hirsi-ali-to-receive-an-honorary-degree-a222e488622f#.s8xilgdyi

[210] "History of the Boycott, Divestment, Sanctions Movement" by Dr. Mitchell Bard. Jewish Virtual Library, February 2016. http://www.jewishvirtuallibrary.org/jsource/anti-semitism/bdshistory.html

[211] Palestinian BDS National Committee, BDS Movement website. https://bdsmovement.net/bnc

tracked employees of three now-defunct organizations: the Holy Land Foundation for Relief and Development, Kind Hearts Foundation for Humanitarian Development, and the Islamic Association for Palestine, all of which were implicated by the federal government for terrorism finance, specifically of Hamas.[212] In his testimony, Schanzer explained that after a Hamas-supporting organization was shut down by the government, it morphed into a new organization operating under a new name, and the officers of the defunct group moved on to continue the mission in the new organizations.

For example, Schanzer reported, several individuals associated with the Holy Land Foundation moved on to work for or on behalf of American Muslims for Palestine (AMP).[213] Among them was Hossein Khatib, a member of AMP's Board, who was previously a Holy Land Foundation regional director. Another, Jamal Said, who was named an unindicted co-conspirator at the Holy Land trial, raised funds for HLF and AMP, and is currently director of the Mosque Foundation, a sponsor of AMP. AMP Board Members Salah Sarsour and Osama Abu Irshaid, also had ties to the Holy Land Foundation (HLF).[214]

AMP is a supporter and facilitator of BDS. According to the NGO Monitor, AMP "supports anti-Israel BDS, accuses Israel of "apartheid," and advocates for a "right of return" and the elimination of Israel: 'Palestinians are more determined than ever to fight on until total liberation, until every refugee can return, until the land of Palestine is free from the river to the sea!'"[215]

BDS Spreads Throughout the West

In 2007, the Palestinian BDS National Committee was founded and became, as the website declares, "the broadest Palestinian civil society coalition that works to lead and support the BDS movement."[216]

In the intervening years, BDS, (which stands for "Boycott, Divestment, Sanctions" against Israel), has established a strong foothold on U.S. campuses,[217] dedicating itself to "withdrawing support for Israel and Israeli and international companies ... [as well as] Israeli sporting, cultural and

---

[212] "Ties between Hamas-linked charities and BDS highlighted in Congressional testimony" By Rebecca Shimoni Stoil. *Times of Israel*, April 20, 2016.
http://www.timesofisrael.com/congressional-testimony-highlights-ties-between-hamas-linked-charities-bds/

[213] Ibid.

[214] American Muslims for Palestine [Profile] NGO Monitor, updated May 23, 2016.
http://www.ngo-monitor.org/ngos/american-muslims-for-palestine-amp/

[215] Ibid.

[216] Palestinian BDS National Committee. https://bdsmovement.net/bnc

[217] "BDS Money Trail Suggests Opaque Funding Network" by Mitchell Bard. The Jewish Week, October 14, 2015. http://www.thejewishweek.com/news/new-york/bds-money-trail-suggests-opaque-funding-network#fbmKV3tMGFGjHluX.99

academic institutions; campaigns urg[ing] banks, local councils, churches, pension funds and universities to withdraw investments from all Israeli companies ... [and] campaigns pressur[ing] governments to fulfill their legal obligation to hold Israel to account, including by ending military trade, free-trade agreements, and expelling Israel from international forums such as the UN and FIFA."[218]

The growing antisemitism on American college campuses today has been fueled by BDS activists, who in turn have received support not only from the Hamas network in the U.S., but from another, unlikely source. The Black Lives Matter (BLM) organization, an aggressive and sometimes violent movement that claims to represent more than 50 black organizations, endorsed BDS in August 2016. As the black movement blended with other belligerent political organizations and moved its anger between college campuses and the streets, the growing aggressiveness of BDS made it a likely partner, and brought Hamas into the center of a growing and hostile movement that took violence into the street. The support that BDS received from this highly visible group resulted in a dramatic growth of support for the Hamas-led movement. Beyond limiting the free speech of those with whom they don't agree, these organizations vehemently oppose efforts to promote peace talks and 'normalization' between Israel and the Palestinians.

CAIR has given open support to BDS and the boycott of Israeli products, despite the fact that such support goes far beyond its own clear mission, as stated on its website: "CAIR's mission is to enhance understanding of Islam, encourage dialogue, protect civil liberties, empower American Muslims, and build coalitions that promote justice and mutual understanding. "

Yet in May 2015, CAIR posted a message on its website, urging Americans to contact their members of Congress to urge them to challenge the passage of the 2015 US-European Union trade bill, which it called anti-BDS legislation. CAIR demanded that the bill be amended to change the language that would penalize European countries opposed to trade with Israel. In this, CAIR reached far beyond its own mission to urge support for a movement designed to destroy a foreign country's economy.[219]

Omar Barghouti, a founding member of the BDS campaign against Israel, explained the endgame for BDS:

> *"A Jewish state in Palestine in any shape or form cannot but contravene the basic rights of the indigenous Palestinian... most definitely we oppose a Jewish state in any part of*

---

[218] "What is BDS?" https://bdsmovement.net/what-is-bds

[219] "Act Today to Defeat Anti-BDS Bill in Congress, May 18, 2015.
https://www.cair.com/press-center/action-alerts/12939-act-today-to-defeat-anti-bds-bill-in-congress.html

Palestine....Ending the occupation doesn't mean anything if it doesn't mean upending the Jewish state itself."[220]

Barghouti was also a founding member of the Palestinian Campaign for the Academic and Cultural Boycott of Israel (PACBI) [221]. This organization operates under the BDS banner but with a different focus, calling on "academics and intellectuals...in the international community to comprehensively and consistently boycott all Israeli academic and cultural institutions..." [222]

Ironically, Barghouti studied at Israel's Tel Aviv University, although the West Bank has 12 universities of its own, East Jerusalem has one, and Gaza has nine. With stunning hypocrisy, Barghouti chose to attend TAU for both his Master's degree and his PhD, although he simultaneously called for a complete cultural and academic boycott of all Israeli academic conferences and promoted boycotts against the Israeli academics and scientists at events outside of Israel. When asked about the apparent conflict, he replied, "My studies at Tel Aviv University are a personal matter and I have no interest in commenting."[223]

The objectives of BDS and Hamas are the same – the ultimate destruction of the state of Israel by every means possible. An interim goal is to silence pro-Israel voices on college campuses in order to weaken American public support for Israel and to make overt anti-Semitism an acceptable form of expression in the U.S.

American Muslims for Palestine (AMP) and Students for Justice in Palestine (SJP)

AMP is another vocal, anti-Israel, pro-Hamas organization, "a Palestinian advocacy group with strong ties to both the US Muslim Brotherhood and the Hamas support infrastructure in the U.S."[224] Founded in 2006 by Dr. Hatem Bazian, a senior lecturer at the University of California-Berkeley and one-time fundraiser for KindHearts, AMP followed in the footsteps of Kindhearts (which replaced Holy Land Foundation), taking over the role of fundraising, propaganda, and lobbying on behalf of

---

[220] "Birds of a Feather? The Link Between BDS and Hamas" by Ziva Dahl. *The Observer*, April 22, 2016. http://observer.com/2016/04/birds-of-a-feather-the-link-between-bds-and-hamas/

[221] https://bdsmovement.net/pacbi

[222] All these were areas captured by Israel after being attacked by Jordan, Syria, and Egypt in the 1967 "Six Day War."

[223] Omar Barghouti Profile, Canary Mission. https://canarymission.org/individuals/omar-barghouti/

[224] "American Muslims for Palestine" The Global Muslim Brotherhood Daily Watch. https://www.globalmbwatch.com/american-muslims-for-palestine/

the Palestinians. It has also become an aggressive actor in the on-campus war against Israel, allying with and supporting BDS.

AMP opened its national offices in Palos Hills, Illinois in 2009. It worked in both the political and financial spheres, claiming to assist thousands of Palestinians "suffering under Israeli aggression."[225]

According to its website, "AMP calls for an end to the Israeli occupation of Palestinian lands, the right of return for Palestinian refugees,[226] an end to Israeli settlement construction and an end to Israel's siege on Gaza. AMP supports the Palestinian call for boycott, divestment and sanctions (BDS) "as a peaceful tool to force Israel to comply with international law."[227] In reality, it is a frontal attack on Israel's existence, threatening to delegitimize the Jewish state by destroying its economy, its international reputation, and, through "right of return," to create demographic disaster..

In his testimony before two joint Congressional subcommittees on terrorist financing, Jonathan Schanzer called AMP a "leading driver of the BDS campaign." AMP is "arguably the most important sponsor and organizer for Students for Justice in Palestine (SJP), which is the most visible arm of the BDS college campaign in the United States," Schanzer said. "AMP provides speakers, training, printed materials, a so-called 'Apartheid Wall,' and grants to SJP activists. AMP even has a campus coordinator on staff whose job is to work directly with SJP and other pro-BDS campus groups across the country. According to an email it sent to subscribers, AMP spent $100,000 on campus activities in 2014 alone." [228]

Benjamin Ryberg, CEO and Director of Research at the Lawfare Project, explains the highly suspect process for receiving funds from the colleges to support these actions: "Funding sources for campus groups are not subject to any disclosure requirements" (unless they are imposed by the individual

---

[225] Ibid

[226] A condition for Middle East peace talks that is required by the PA and Hamas is the "right of return" to cities in Israel for Palestinians, who claim they were driven out of their homes in Israel's 1948 War of Independence, *and their descendants*. When UNRWA began operations in 1950, it was responding to the needs of about 750,000 Palestine refugees. UNRWA defines the Palestinian 'right of return' as "persons whose normal place of residence was Palestine during the period 1 June 1946 to 15 May 1948, and who lost both home and means of livelihood as a result of the 1948 conflict." Today, some 5 million Palestine 'refugees' claim the 'right of return', although only 30,000 – 50,000 original refugees were still alive in 2012. UNRWA continues to operate 58 'refugee' camps for Palestinians in Jordan, Lebanon, the Syrian Arab Republic, the Gaza Strip and the West Bank, including East Jerusalem. Source: https://www.unrwa.org/palestine-refugees. "Various estimates put the number of Arab refugees in 1948 was between 538,000 (Israeli sources), 720,000 (UN estimates) and 850,000 (Palestinian sources). Source: http://www.jewishvirtuallibrary.org/do-palestinian-refugees-have-a-legal-quot-right-of-return-quot-to-israel

[227] http://www.ampalestine.org/about-amp

[228] "Former Treasury Official: Same Network That Funded Hamas in U.S. Backs Boycotts of Israel"

universities at which the groups are operating).[229] The Lawfare Project[230] tracks what it calls "the politicization of human rights." Ryberg maintains that most of the identifiable resources for student groups such as SJP and the Muslim Student Association (MSA) come from student funds distributed by the student government or another campus agency. Typically, the only requirement is that they present a request with a budget reflecting their needs; they need not document any other items, neither expenses nor revenues.[231]

SJP, which has some 170 independent chapters throughout the U.S., is one of the primary organizers of anti-Israel activities on college campuses. Founded in 2001 at the University of California, Berkeley, SJP has become the leading pro-Palestinian, anti-Israel voice on campus. AMP is its primary sponsor and supporter.

In March 2014, AMP joined five other American Islamic groups – the Council on American-Islamic Relations (CAIR), the Muslim American Society (MAS), the Islamic Circle of North America (ICNA), the Muslim Legal Fund of America (MLFA), and the Mosque Foundation. The new coalition was called the U.S. Council of Muslim Organizations (USCMO). It claims to be "the largest coalition of national, regional, and local Muslim organizations" whose purpose is "to create and sustain an urgent, collective sense of direction that well-serves the American Muslim community toward the betterment and guidance of our nation," and "to serve as a representative voice for Muslims as that faith community seeks to enhance its positive impact on society."[232] The double meaning implicit in those words is stunning.

The closely interconnected relationships among the members of USCMO are clear. All are tied to Hamas and the Muslim Brotherhood. Board members include the leaders of AMP, CAIR, ICNA, and MAS, all of which are Brotherhood-sponsored organizations.[233] A network of men who are linked to Hamas-supporting, Brotherhood-sponsored organizations is also clear, as Jonathan Schanzer explained. His research tracked employees of three organizations – the Holy Land Foundation for Relief and Development, Kind Hearts Foundation for Humanitarian Development and the Islamic

---

[229] "BDS Money Trail Suggests Opaque Funding Network" by Mitchell Bard. October 13, 2015. *Jewish Week*http://www.thejewishweek.com/news/new-york/bds-money-trail-suggests-opaque-funding-network#fbmKV3tMGFGjHluX.99

[230] www.thelawfareproject.org

[231] The MSA was founded by the Muslim Brotherhood in the U.S. in 1963 at the University of Illinois. It in turn founded the Islamic Society of North America (ISNA). Both organization were listed as like-minded organizations in the "Memorandum" (See Appendix II) and as co-conspirators in the Holy Land Foundation trial (see Appendix IV).

[232] USCMO official website. http://www.uscmo.org/about-us/

[233] Executive Team http://www.uscmo.org/board-members/

Association for Palestine — all of which are now defunct. All three were implicated in federal cases relating to the financing of Hamas.

Schanzer found that seven key employees of these organizations had moved into positions associated with the Illinois-based organization American Muslims for Palestine (AMP). [234]

A brief look at several members of the AMP board illustrates the point:

- Dr. Osama Abuirshaid, for example, AMP's National Policy Director, was editor of IAP's Arabic periodical, Al-Zaitounah, which earlier promoted Hamas and published advertisements by terrorist-affiliated charities like the Holy Land Foundation, the Global Relief Foundation, and the Benevolence International Foundation.

- Salah Sarsour, now an officer of AMP, was cited by the FBI[235] for his fundraising activities for Hamas through the Holy Land Foundation.

- Yousef Shahin, who is also a member of AMP's National Board, was once president of the Islamic Association for Palestine (IAP) in New Jersey, precursor to CAIR.

- Taher Herzallah, AMP's Associate Director of Outreach & Grassroots Organizing, proudly calls himself one of the "Irvine 11". In 2014, Herzallah posted photos to his Facebook page showing wounded Israeli soldiers and a burning tank, under which he wrote, "The most beautiful site in my eyes."[236]

- Abdelbaset Hamayel, who is a registered agent for AMP, was Executive Director and Secretary General for the Islamic Association for Palestine (IAP). He also represented KindHearts in Illinois and Wisconsin.

And so it goes. While the organizations accused of supporting terrorist groups may be gone, in true Muslim Brotherhood fashion, they have been replaced by new organizations with new names to carry on the work they left unfinished. Tactics have changed but the underlying missions – the destruction of Israel and civilization jihad in the U.S. continue.

---

[234] "Investigation Exposes AMP Leaders' Ties to Former U.S-Based Hamas-Support Network" Investigative Project, June 24, 2015.
http://www.investigativeproject.org/4891/investigation-exposes-amp-leaders-ties-to-former

[235] "Investigation Exposes AMP Leaders' Ties to Former U.S-Based Hamas-Support Network" Investigative Project, June 24, 2015.
http://www.investigativeproject.org/4891/investigation-exposes-amp-leaders-ties-to-former

[236] "AMP Official Defends Hamas, Praises Israeli Casualties" by IPT News. July 21, 2014.
http://www.investigativeproject.org/4470/amp-official-defends-hamas-praises-israeli

Supporting the Hamas Agenda

The underlying scope of BDS' aims is extremely broad, and supports the ultimate mission of Hamas. The purpose of BDS is not only to harm Israel economically, but ultimately to destroy the Jewish state by destabilizing its economy and delegitimizing Israel in the eyes of the world.

"In the case of divestment, this primarily takes the form of non-binding resolutions by student groups and lobbying to remove Israeli companies from university investment portfolios. Support for BDS is also expressed during Israel Apartheid Week programming, at rallies, and surrounding "guerilla theater" events such as mock checkpoints that ignore terror attacks. BDS on campus is often masked by a façade of respectability and intellectual rigor, for instance in pseudo-academic conferences that advance an anti-Israel agenda."[237]

Among the most notorious chapters of BDS on campus are:

- The University of Chicago, home to a highly active BDS campus movement, U of C Divest. With the support of over 20 student organizations on the campus, the organization has succeeded in passing a BDS resolution in Chicago's student government. In the process, it defeated an amendment that supported the continued self-determination of the Jewish people and the existence of the sovereign state of Israel.[238]

- At the University of California-Davis, the student senate also voted to divest itself of companies that do business with Israel. After the vote, a proponent of the move and a student senator herself, Student Senator Azka Fayyaz posted on her Facebook page "Hamas and Shariah law have taken over UC Davis."

- At Vassar College in Poughkeepsie, NY, supporters of BDS were successful in passing a BDS resolution on campus in early 2016. Vassar's Students for Justice in Palestine (SJP) sold T-shirts with the photograph of anti-Israel terrorist, airplane hijacker, and

---

[237] "BDS (Boycotts, Divestment, and Sanctions)" http://www.ngo-monitor.org/key-issues/bds/tactics/#campusactivity

[238] "University Of Chicago Champions Hamas-Driven BDS Movement"Frontpagemag.com , October 20, 2016 http://www.frontpagemag.com/fpm/264556/university-chicago-champions-hamas-driven-bds-frontpagemagcom

PFLP[239] figurehead Leila Khaled holding a gun, and imprinted with the words "Resistance is not Terrorism."[240]

The Vassar BDS website provides a list of "BDS Successes in US Schools" The list includes universities and colleges throughout the country. The students who actively come out for BDS and other anti-Israel activities are generally connected to such groups as Students for Justice in Palestine (SJP), the Muslim Student Association (MSA), and American Muslims for Palestine (AMP), all offspring of the Muslim Brotherhood and supporters of Hamas.[241]

- At Portland State University,[242] Ami Horowitz, a filmmaker known for his revealing 'man on the street' interviews, posed as a representative from "American Friends for Hamas." His questions not only elicited favorable responses regarding Hamas, but in the process, he raised hundreds of dollars in donations from feckless college students who were willing to support Hamas through a fake organization they had never heard of before. Horowitz explained that the money would help Hamas in its program of bombing schools, places of worship, shopping centers, hospitals, cafes, and other "soft targets," attacks that would not only "destroy Israel" but would "wipe Israel off the map ... We're not your father's terrorist organization," he said. "We're kind of rebuilt and re-branded ... It's BDS at the next level. There's BDS and we're like, BDS plus."[243]

Horowitz' spoof lifted the veil hiding the low level of information afflicting so many young, supposedly educated Americans. Either the subjects of his spoof were truly uninformed about Hamas or they had already been subjected to and convinced by the campaign of hate perpetrated by groups like BDS. The collaboration of Hamas-supporting organizations like BDS, Black Lives Matter, and the Muslim Brotherhood have created a culture of hate and class warfare that bodes ill for America.

On a refreshing note, on April 20, 2017, Tufts University cast a resounding blow against this bigotry when its Board of Trustees rejected a

---

[239] PFLP is the acronym for the Palestinian Front for the Liberation of Palestine

[240] "Orgs split on how to show Israel-Palestine solidarity" by Stoddard Meigs on February 17, 2016 http://miscellanynews.org/2016/02/17/features/orgs-split-on-how-to-show-israel-palestine-solidarity/

[241] "From the River to the Sea..." October 31, 2014 HamasOnCampus.org
http://www.hamasoncampus.org/single-post/2014/11/01/From-the-River-to-the-Sea

[242] College students agree to make donations to Hamas - YouTube May 23, 2016
https://www.youtube.com/watch?v=DQklj7M_ygY

[243] *Ibid*

bid from the 11-member Student Senate to "divest from four companies—Elbit Systems, G4S, Hewlett Packard Enterprise, and Northrop Grumman—that they claimed are implicated in the "occupation" and "apartheid" of "Occupied Palestinian territory."[244] In a campus-wide e-mail, Board Chair Peter R. Dolan wrote, "Tufts University will not divest from the companies doing business in Israel or impose criteria that would preclude investments in such companies. ... Tufts University should not take institutional positions on matters of politics and public affairs unless they relate directly to our core academic mission."[245]

Overall, however, the current climate on many college campuses today that have been targeted by Hamas-supporting organizations is intolerant, increasingly antisemitic, and in opposition to the most basic American principles embodied in the Constitution. It demonstrates how far the Muslim Brotherhood's efforts at civilization jihad have already succeeded.

From Rhetoric to Disorder to Anarchy – Playing into the Hands of Terrorists

By the beginning of February 2016, the speeches and disruptions had become demonstrations in the streets, which in turn erupted into anarchy and violence. The same groups that had joined forces with Hamas-supporting organizations on campus, to disrupt and demonstrate against those with whom it disagreed, now took to the streets.

On the evening of February 1, the University of California-Berkeley exploded with the ill-informed rage and accompanying violence of local college students and professional agitators imported for the occasion. These were not spontaneous events, but rather well-orchestrated protests, organized among many groups and well-paid activists. Their riots were programmed in real time through social media. The following night, similar demonstrations erupted at New York University, similarly organized.

At Berkeley, ironically the home to the free speech movement of the 1960s, the 'anti-fascists' stormed the police barricades and manned their Twitter posts to ensure that the Republicans would not be able to hear their speaker, Breitbart's Milo Yiannopoulos.

One tweeter posted the following: "@OccupyOakland ...immediately! San Diego, California Friends and familia - Heads up! #BorderPatrol #checkpoint near Camp Pendleton is active." In a later tweet, she wrote, "We won this night. We will control the streets. We will liberate the land.

---

[244] "Tufts chairman shoots down demands for Israel boycott" by Kassy Dillon. CampusReform.org, April 20, 2017.
https://www.campusreform.org/?ID=9086

[245] Ibid

We will fight fascists. We will dismantle the state. This is war." In short, the so-called "anti-fascists" employed fascist tactics to ensure that the right of free speech would not prevail at UC Berkeley.

Another tweeter, posting the next day under the name Occupy Oakland, sent her comrades to a new location to confront police, saying, "#TheVillage get down to 36th and MLK #Oakland NOW dozens of cops trying to kick out residents of tiny home village. #HomesNow #resist."

Demonstration at the University of California-Berkeley

Occupy Oakland was created in October 2011 as a part of the Occupy Wall Street movement. Many of its participants were paid agitators, responding to ads on CraigsList.com and paid to stay and disrupt normal commerce for days and weeks. In February 1, 2012, Occupy Oakland overwhelmingly endorsed a proposal in support of the BDS movement against Israel.[246] The vote was 135-1 with 4 abstentions, thus bringing Hamas into the growing movement of college activists and anarchists.

The connections between BDS and Hamas are clear and close. The alliances between BDS and other agitating groups such as Occupy Oakland, Black Lives Matter, and a host of other anti-Israel, anti-Trump gangs and anarchist groups therefore provide Hamas with an easy avenue into the heart of hardcore disrupters, helping Hamas to work its way into the very

---

[246] "Occupy Oakland votes 135-1 to support BDS". By Emma Silvers. Jweekly, 9 Feb 2012. http://www.jweekly.com/2012/02/10/occupy-oakland-votes-135-1-to-support-bds/

fabric of the anarchy that is taking over college campuses and spilling out onto urban streets.

'Islamizing' American Universities

Increasingly, American universities are demonstrating their appetite for 'diversity' by hiring Muslim professors, even those who espouse jihad and shariah. In an interview with Global Patriot Radio on September 14, 2016, Cinnamon Stillwell, the West Coast representative of the Middle East Forum's Campus Watch, spoke of this when discussing her campaign to compel San Francisco State University to cancel its memorandum of understanding (MOU) with An-Najah University in the West Bank. "They endow chairs, they have summer programs where they bring in professors to speak and take part in their educational programs. As you may know, their motto—and they're very open about their stated goal—is the 'Islamization of knowledge.'"[247]

Hatem Bazian speaking at a demonstration

Each year, for example, UC Berkeley professor Hatem Bazian, co-founder of both, Students for Justice in Palestine (SJP) in 2001, and AMP in 2006, leads the Islamophobia Research and Documentation Project (IRDP), which is housed at the university's Center for Race and Gender. The IRDP purports to "[focus] on a systematic and empirical approach to the study of Islamophobia and its impact on the American Muslim community ... by bringing together academics, thinkers, practitioners and researchers from around the globe who engage, question and challenge the existing disparities in economic, political, social and cultural relations."[248]

Writing on the project's website, however, Bazian uses Islamophobia (which he calls "otherizing") as a tool for incitement. He describes "otherizing" as "state sanctioned targeting of individuals and communities, intensive surveillance and securitization, tailored forms of legal restrictions, modes of civil society exclusion, heightened restriction of movement, and

---

[247] "Infiltrating Islamists and Palestinian Extremism in U.S. Universities" Global Patriot Radio, September 14, 2016. http://www.meforum.org/6301/cinnamon-stillwell-campus-watch-on-sfsu-scandal

[248] "Islamophobia Research & Documentation Project" http://crg.berkeley.edu/content/islamophobia

an elite and corporate induced barrage of negative media entanglement. ... Muslims and Islam are an otherized category in the U.S. with multipronged levels of exclusion and forms of racialized discrimination inflicted upon individuals and groups. The othering process directed at Muslims was unleashed by rightwing political elites that wanted to craft a strategy to contest power in a post-Cold War era." [249]

Not surprisingly, the program is co-sponsored by CAIR. Bazian is also a co-founder and Professor of Islamic Law and Theology at Zaytuna College, which claims to be the first Accredited Muslim Liberal Arts College in the United States.

Even as a student at SFU, Bazian's antisemitic positions were clear. As president of SFSU Associated Students, the Student Union Governing Board, and The General Union of Palestinian Students (GUPS), Bazian battled against SFU's Jewish students. In one instance, he prevented the appointment of a Jewish student to SFSU's Student Judicial Council "on grounds that the individual supported the state of Israel and was therefore, by definition, a racist."[250]

The Canary Mission[251] called Bazian "the Most Dangerous Professor in America, saying, "Bazian is a chameleon. In the academic world, he is slick and intellectual. In his writings he has a sophisticated anti-Zionist narrative that delegitimizes the Jewish people's history, identity and connection to Israel...[A]t rallies the veneer falls away and we see his crude racist rhetoric — a rhetoric that is aggressive and pro-violence."[252]

Although he denies having advocated violence, once at a rally at Berkeley in April 2004, he asked the crowd, "Are you angry? Are you angry? Are you angry? We've been watching intifada in Palestine, we've been watching an uprising in Iraq....[A]nd the question is that, what are we doing? How come we don't have an intifada in this country...and it's about time that we have an intifada in this country that changes fundamentally the political dynamics in here [sic]. And we know...they're gonna say it's some Palestinian being too radical, well you haven't seen radicalism yet!"[253]

At San Francisco State University, Professor Rabab Abdulhadi, who once taught at Bir Zeit University in the West Bank, is the director of the

---

[249] http://crg.berkeley.edu/content/islamophobia

[250] Hatem Bazian (profile) https://canarymission.org/professors/hatem-bazian/

[251] An anonymous website "created to document the people and groups that are promoting hatred of the USA, Israel and Jews on college campuses in North America" http://canarymission.org

[252] "Berkeley "Intifada" by Malcolm A. Kline Accuracy in Academia, June 4, 2004. https://www.academia.org/berkeley-intifada/

[253] Covert Watchdog Calls Founder of Students for Justice in Palestine 'Most Dangerous Professor in America' by Rachel Frommer. July12, 2017. https://canarymission.org/professors/hatem-bazian/

Arab and Muslim Ethnicities and Diaspora Initiative, an early ethnic studies program devoted to Arab and Muslim studies. She is one of the founders of an openly anti-Israel and pro-Palestinian terrorism group called the U.S. Campaign for the Academic and Cultural Boycott of Israel.[254]

These are only two of a growing list of devout shariah-supremacist staff entering the faculties of formerly main line colleges and universities throughout the country, and slowly but effectively politicizing the education of their students with a toxic anti-Israel, pro-Palestinian agenda. The growing intolerance on America's college campuses today leads directly back to the doorsteps of these highly politicized faculties that brook no argument against their personal opinions and promote agendas of political activism against Israel, Zionism, and free speech that does not coincide with their pro-Palestinian agendas.

The confluence and commingling of so many movements with different and sometimes competing missions, whose energy and ginned-up rage is now filling our universities and our cities across the country, pose a growing danger to the U.S. The inclusion of Hamas-linked groups increases the danger by opening the door to a new avenue through which to carry out their mission to destroy America.

Other Enablers of the Muslim Brotherhood's Civilization Jihad Agenda

The support for civilization Jihad is personified by **Linda Sarsour**, executive director of the Arab American Association of New York (AAANY), and a leader of the Women's March on Washington, that took place on January 21, 2017, one day after Donald Trump's inauguration. Her method of operation is to personally involve herself in as many activist progressive groups as she can and link them all to Palestine and the promotion of rights for Muslims. Former President Barack Obama's White House called her a "champion of change," and CAIR awarded their first "American Muslim of the Year" award to her in 2013.[255] Since then she has been "parroting talking points fed to her by the Muslim Brotherhood contingent within CAIR."[256]

Why is this important? In an article published by ClarionProject.org,[257] Meira Svirsky explained, "Sarsour, a Palestinian activist, is the darling of the

---

[254] Ibid

[255] "Fake Activist Exposed: The Real Linda Sarsour." Ikhras.com, May 10, 2016 http://ikhras.com/fake-activist-exposed-the-real-linda-sarsour/

[256] Ibid

[257] "Truth and Deception: Calling Out Linda Sarsour on Al Aqsa" by Meira Svirsky. ClarionProjectorg, July 24, 2017 https://clarionproject.org/truth-deceptions-calling-linda-sarsour/

left, the feminist movement, and the BDS movement. Information she spreads is taken at face value; no one usually bothers to check the facts. Because of this, her comments matter."

At the Women's March in Washington, she called for support for the Palestinian woman, about whom she said, "you can count on [her], your Palestinian Muslim sister, to keep her voice loud."[258]

True to form, Sarsour also latched on to the Standing Rock demonstration in Cannon Ball, North Dakota,[259] protesting against the construction of the Dakota Access Pipeline. She carried the 'Palestine' flag, although it had nothing to do with the issue at hand.

Sarsour, who was born in Brooklyn of Palestinian parents, is a family member of Hamas operatives, who have spent time in Israeli jails for their connections to terrorist activities.[260] Nevertheless, Sarsour achieved a rapid rise to prominence and became the darling of the feminist movement as an outspoken advocate for what she calls "the rights of all women." In a November 2016 tweet, she wrote, "We can disagree & still love each other, unless your disagreement is rooted in my oppression & denial of my humanity and right to exist."

Linda Sarsour at Dakota Access Pipeline demonstration

Yet, by her own reckoning, "all women" does not include Zionists or Israeli women, who she says cannot be feminists. She is vehemently anti-Israel and a fervent supporter of the BDSmovement. She once tweeted "nothing is creepier than Zionism." And where she demands her own "right to exist," she would happily deny that right to Israel and to the six and a half million Israeli Jews who live there.

Sarsour enjoys wide support for her activism from the political left, and like her supporters, she tosses the arrows of "Islamophobia" at

---

[258] "Van Ness: Linda Sarsour, Women's March Organizer and Fake Feminist" by Alex Vanness, Febuary 3, 2017. https://counterjihadreport.com/2017/02/04/vanness-linda-sarsour-womens-march-organizer-and-fake-feminist/

[259] Ibid

[260] "Linda Sarsour And Her Family Ties To Hamas- GMBDW Reported First On Women's March on Washington Organizer" by GMBWatch, January 25, 2017.
https://www.globalmbwatch.com/2017/01/25/correction-linda-sasours-family-ties-to-hamas-operatives-cannot-be-substantiated/

everyone who challenges her. On January 23, 2017, the Southern Poverty Law Center (SPLC) gratuitously tweeted, "Islamophobes have been attacking #WomensMarch organizer @lsarsour. We stand with her against this type of hate and bigotry. #IMarchWithLinda"[261]

At a Jewish Voice for Peace summit, she sat next to convicted terrorist Rasmea Odeh, a former member of PFLP[262] who was responsible for a 1969 terrorist attack in an Israeli supermarket which killed two Jewish students.

Leon Kaner and Edward Joffee, who died in a 1969 bombing at the hands of PFLP terrorist Rasmea Odeh.

Odeh was released in a prisoner exchange, after serving only ten years of a lifetime sentence, and later emigrated to the U.S. It was to this woman that Sarsour gave a warm hug, and of who she said that she was "honored and privileged to be here in this space, and honored to be on this stage with Rasmea."[263]

On July 7, 2017, CAIR rushed to support Sarsour, and posted on its website an endorsement entitled "CAIR Calls for #IStandWithLinda 'Push Back' Against Smear Campaign Targeting Linda Sarsour." The text read, "The Council on American-Islamic Relations (CAIR), the nation's largest Muslim civil rights and advocacy organization, today called on people of all faiths and backgrounds to "push back" against an online smear campaign targeting Linda Sarsour -- a nationally-known and respected Muslim community activist -- using #IStandWithLinda."

Sarsour opposes American Laws for American Courts (ALAC). And she supports shariah, which she explained in a 2011 tweet: "shariah law is reasonable and once u read into the details it makes a lot of sense." In a January 20017 Tweet, she went even further, writing, "There is NOT ONE example of Muslims trying to impose Sharia on ANY ONE. No legislations. Anti-Muslim rallies playing on the gullible." Denying history and the current practices in such countries as Saudi Arabia, Pakistan, Afghanistan, Malaysia, Indonesia, to mention only a few, Sarsour creates her own facts to fit her current narrative.

---

[261] "The Southern Poverty Law Center (SPLC) defended Linda Sarsour"
https://www.infowars.com/splc-defends-pro-shariah-womens-march-organizer/

[262] Popular Front for the Liberation of Palestine

[263] "Linda Sarsour And Her 'Mentor'" Counter Jihad Report, July 7, 2017.
https://counterjihadreport.com/tag/siraj-wahhaj/

She speaks against the barbaric custom of female genital mutilation (FGM), but she claims that FGM has nothing to do with Islam, despite the ample evidence that this brutal practice, most often carried out on small children, is explicitly approved, condoned, or obligated in both Shi'a and Sunni Islamic Law (based on relevant hadiths). Once again, she makes up her 'truth'

Even as she has been outspoken about women's rights, she curses others fighting the same battles, including activists for women such as Ayaan Hirsi Ali, who was herself a victim of FGM at the age of five, in the most vulgar terms. [264] Hirsi Ali is a champion of the rights of women, particularly Muslim women, and speaks out boldly against FGM and its widespread practice in Muslim communities.

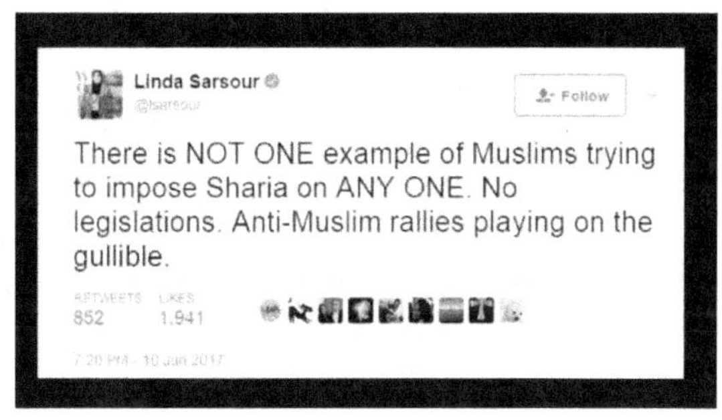

Sarsour's hypocrisy is transparent, but that does not keep her from carrying on with her crusade, and making up her facts as she goes along. That she is not only accepted but lionized in liberal activist circles is more evidence that her message, however crude, false, and hypocritical, is reaching an audience that accepts her ideas and is caught up in the raw emotion of her message.

Her rhetoric reached a feverish pitch in July 2017, when she spoke at the annual banquet of the Islamic Society of America (ISNA). ISNA is the largest Muslim organization in North America and serves as an umbrella organization for many Islamic groups and mosques around the country. In her speech, Sarsour claimed as her inspiration and "favorite person in this room" Imam Siraj Wahhaj,[265] whom Sarsour calls a "mentor, motivator, and encourager" and who called for jihad against the Trump administration.

"And our beloved prophet ... said to him, 'A word of truth in front of a tyrant ruler or leader, that is the best form of jihad,'" Sarsour said.

"I hope that ... when we stand up to those who oppress our communities, that Allah accepts from us that as a form of jihad, that we are struggling against tyrants and rulers not only abroad in the Middle East or on the other side of the world, but here in

---

[264] In her 2011 tweet, she wrote about Aayan Hirsi Ali and Brigitte Gabriel: "I wish I could take their vaginas away – they don't deserve to be women."

[265] Siraj Wahhaj was listed as an unindicted co-conspirator in the 1993 Wrld Trade Center bombing, led by convicted terrorists

these United States of America, where you have fascists and white supremacists and Islamophobes reigning in the White House."[266]

Although Sarsour later insisted she was talking only about a "jihad of words," her comments raised a storm of condemnation over the possibility that she was calling for a holy war against the Trump administration. ISNA showed its support for her in a statement by its president, Azhar Azeez, who said on behalf of the organization, "ISNA is proud to provide a platform for the exchange of ideas put forward by speakers such as Linda Sarsour. We appreciate Linda's commitment to social justice and look forward to hosting her at future ISNA events."

Sarsour is an example of how a single individual, even one allied with terrorists and whose statements are patently self-serving lies, can elevate her own position by blatantly seizing the microphone, blasting her message to anyone who will listen, and garnering the support with known terror supporters and anti-American activists. The standing ovation she received at CUNY where she gave the 2017 commencement speech is testimony to the threat that she represents.

The Southern Poverty Law Center

One of the most insidious and vicious of the groups supporting the goals of Hamas in the U.S. is the Southern Poverty Law Center (SPLC). Once an icon for racial tolerance and equality, the group was active in the civil rights movement of the 1950s and 1960s. But over time it transformed itself into what it has now become: a vicious, nationally active hate group that has amassed an incredible fortune by selling fear. Its mission today, as it appears on its website, is to "monitor hate groups and other extremists throughout the United States and expose their activities to the public, the media, and law enforcement." [267] Its modus operandi is to brand conservative and religious groups and individuals throughout America as "hate groups," pandering in fear-mongering to its wealthy sponsors and to the general American population.

The SPLC claims to promote tolerance, even as it demonizes, with the intent to destroy, those with whom it disagrees. It lumps conservatives, religious organizations representing what they call the "Christian right" (such as the Family Research Council, Concerned Women for America, and the American Family Association), and anti-terrorist think tanks (such as the Investigative Project, the Center for Security Policy, and the Clarion

---

[266] "Muslim activist Linda Sarsour's reference to 'jihad' draws conservative wrath" by Samantha Schmidt. Washington Post, July 7, 2017.
https://www.washingtonpost.com/news/morning-mix/wp/2017/07/07/muslim-activist-linda-sarsours-reference-to-jihad-draws-conservative-wrath/?utm_term=.fbf3ab3d0610

[267] "Fighting Hate" https://www.splcenter.org/fighting-hate

Project) with neo-Nazis and Ku Klux Klan chapters, and calls them all "hate groups." It links organizations like Third Reich Books, the White Aryan Resistance, and the notorious Westboro Baptist Church, with groups that champion American patriotism, conservative religious conviction, an abiding respect for the U.S. Constitution, and a firm belief in the rule of law. They include the Center for Security Policy, the David Horowitz Freedom Center, American Border Patrol, the Clarion Center, Citizens for National Security, Jihad Watch, Refugee Resettlement Watch, Team America Political Action Committee, Americans for Legal Immigration (ALIPAC), and the Center for Immigration Studies, among others.

The SPLC claims to promote justice while taking upon itself the authority of judge and jury, deciding who is a "hater," and offering neither due process nor a fair hearing for its targets. Meanwhile, it makes money hand-over-fist by sowing the seeds of fear and incitement. In its 2016 Annual Report, the SPLC reported its total endowment fund assets to be $319,283,961,[268] making it by far the wealthiest "civil rights" organization in the country.

While claiming on its website to be "dedicated to reducing prejudice," and "improving intergroup relations," its underlying mission is crystal clear. This was clearly articulated by Mark Potok, its former spokesman, at a 2007 event in Michigan, where Potok, said "Sometimes the press will describe us as monitoring hate groups, I want to say plainly that our aim in life is to destroy these groups, completely destroy them."[269] Not surprisingly, the far left Huffington Post called Potok "a leader in one of the most highly regarded operations monitoring the extreme right in the world today."[270]

In its efforts to destroy those it considers its enemies, the SPLC has created what it calls "A Hate Map," which it publicizes on its website and in the press. By mid-2017, this interactive map displayed and listed the names and locations of 917 organizations it branded as "hate groups."

The list of "hate groups" is accompanied by a list of hundreds of "extremists" and a more detailed list which singles out fifteen high profile "anti-Muslim extremists." The abbreviated list is composed of those it thinks are most dangerous, among the hundreds of others it has labeled as extremists. They are: Ann Corcoran (*Refugee Resettlement Watch*), Steven Emerson (*Investigative Project*), Brigitte Gabriel (*ACT! for America*), Frank Gaffney (*Center for Security Policy*), Pamela Geller (*American Freedom Defense Initiative*), John Guandolo (*Understanding the Threat*), Ayaan Hirsi

---

[268] 2016 Annual Report.
https://www.splcenter.org/sites/default/files/com_splc_annual_report_2016-2017web.pdf

[269] "Southern Poverty Law Center: 'Our Aim in Life Is to Destroy These Groups, Completely'" by Tyler O'Neil September 1, 2017 https://pjmedia.com/trending/2017/09/01/southern-poverty-law-center-our-aim-in-life-is-to-destroy-these-groups-completely/

[270] "Mark Potok" http://www.huffingtonpost.com/author/mark-potok

Ali (*author, former member of the Dutch parliament, and activist against female genital mutilation*), David Horowitz (*Front Page Magazine*), Ryan Mauro (*Clarion Project*), Maajid Nawaz (*British activist and author*), Robert Muise (*American Freedom Law Center*), Daniel Pipes (*Middle East Forum*), Walid Shoebat (*Shoebat Foundation*), and Robert Spencer (*Jihad Watch*).

On June 9, 2015, SPLC published an edition of its magazine *Intelligence Report* in which it listed its "dirty dozen" of "the most hardline anti-Muslim women activists in America." In an article called "Women Against Islam," it singled out such outspoken conservative women as Ann Coulter, Laura Ingraham, Clare Lopez, Judge Jeanine Pirro, and Diana West, as well as Pamela Geller and Brigitte Gabriel, whom the SPLC called "professional provocateurs" and "Muslim bashers."[271] The article represented a virtual hit list of women who have the courage to speak out against the civilization jihad that threatens America today.

A year later, on October 25, 2016, the SPLC went even further when it published "A Journalist's Manual: Field Guide to Anti-Muslim extremists,"[272] in which it created a black list of conservative and religious leaders. The list contains Muslims, Christians, and Jews, scholars, and activists. All are active in the fight against the threat of Islamic jihad and the encroachment of shariah in America. Several among them have themselves been victims of Islamic hatred and violence. Like Linda Sarsour, the SPLC makes up its own 'truths' and broadcasts its venom without regard for the damage it causes to freedom in this country or to the lives and work of its targets and their organizations.

It claims to be monitoring over 1,600 "extremist groups" throughout the US, and has mounted a campaign to systematically destroy as many of those organizations and their leaders as possible. In late August 2017, SPLC cashed in on the erupting Antifa/Black Lives Matter street violence and expanded its website to include a new map showing more than 1,500 Confederacy-linked statues throughout the country and a list of towns, cities, counties, and even schools named after Confederate leaders, warning that these statues and institutions have "the potential to unleash more turmoil and bloodshed." In doing so, the organization crossed the dangerously thin line between rabble-rousing and incitement to violence.

At this writing, SPLC remains an organization that makes its money calling out what it claims to see as "hate rhetoric," but continues to be tone deaf to its own hate-filled message, spewing lies and venom as it tries to destroy its victims. Despite its active role as a hate-monger, the SPLC still

---

[271] *Intelligence Report* "Southern Poverty Law Center, October 9, 2015.
https://www.splcenter.org/fighting-hate/intelligence-report/2015/women-against-islam
[272] "A Journalist's Manual: Field Guide to Anti-Muslim Extremists"
https://www.splcenter.org/20161025/journalists-manual-field-guide-anti-muslim-extremists

enjoys status and wide support from the general press, and still gets high ratings from the organizations that evaluate not-for-profit organizations.

But it may only be a matter of time before SPLC falls victim to its own agenda. The excesses of its attacks upon good people have raised the ire of a broad spectrum of Americans, including its targets, who have already begun to fight back. In 2017, the first lawsuit for defamation against the SPLC was filed against it by Maajid Nawaz, who presents himself as a former jihadi, but whom they called an "anti-Muslim extremist." More lawsuits and other forms or response have already begun to follow as a growing anger over the SPLC false and defamatory accusations continues to grow.

Part V

Civilization Jihad – Using Our Best American Instincts Against Us

The growing violence in the demonstrations on campus and in the street fits comfortably into the Brotherhood's program of civilization jihad, confusing and conflating issues in an increasingly complex network of alliances. This comes right out of the Brotherhood playbook. It generates the chaos and violence associated with the unrest, but is wrapped in the protective mantle of political correctness that calls any opposition to its agenda "Islamophobia." Anyone opposing its agenda is branded an Islamophobe.

The duplicity that underlies the practice of Civilization Jihad has made it possible for the Muslim Brotherhood and its network of supporting organizations to make significant headway in its mission, with little resistance from mainstream America. On the contrary, the mainstream seems to have largely embraced the calls for 'diversity', and distanced itself from anything that can be branded Islamophobic. In the growing disorder that is fast becoming a dangerously volatile environment on American universities and city streets, the Brotherhood has found feckless collaborators who are more than willing to help lay the groundwork for Islamization.

Their growing hysteria in the quest for 'diversity' and their need to protect Muslims against perceived 'Islamophobia' have stifled free speech and limited the right of Americans to discuss real issues relating to the role of Islam in America. This is one of the outcomes of civilization jihad, and proof of how successful the Brotherhood's civilization jihad has been. The substantial amount of documentation that is now available about the Brotherhood's alliances with Hamas-supporting organizations allows for little doubt that the Muslim Brotherhood's agenda in America is a real and growing threat to the values that are the core of American society.

The discovery of the "Explanatory Memorandum" and "Islamic Action for Palestine – An internal memo" both reveal the intent of Muslim Brotherhood organizations to redefine America as an Islamic country. The recorded transcript of the Philadelphia conference, and the consistently virulent rhetoric at Muslim events, where keynote speakers are known terrorists, terrorist supporters, and agitators, further demonstrate the Brotherhood's mission to destabilize and destroy the foundations of the American Republic. Yet all the documents that have been discovered, and the court cases that have verified their authenticity, have amounted to little in the eyes of the average American. That so many Americans can ignore the evidence and embrace the diversity script makes this increasingly chaotic movement a threat to America's future.

> "CAIR has been both the creator and the continuing facilitator for the ongoing process of civilization jihad as it "demands that employers fire any employee that "defames Islam"; it engages in company-wide boycotts (rather than just boycotting the product in question), false name-calling such as "Islamophobe" or "bigot," calls on its membership to flood companies with phone calls, emails and letters, amounting to harassment so companies cannot get work done, embarks on public campaigns maligning companies and individuals, lobbies in Congress against any legislation that would protect America from Islamic terrorism, and infiltrates governmental agencies, societal institutions, and school boards in order to advance its Islamist agenda. It provides disinformation, misinformation, and intentionally deceives the public about its true nature, its agenda, and the Islamist threat generally."[273]

CAIR's bag of tricks is full and it uses them to obfuscate, deceive, and overpower the opposition in order to Islamize and impose shariah in America. Here are a few of their tactics:

Jihad by Interfaith Outreach

On the morning of Saturday, January 21, 2017, one day after the inauguration of President Donald Trump, the long-held tradition of an interfaith prayer service was held at the Washington National Cathedral. Representatives of many faiths recited prayers, some in English, some in their native languages, for the new President and for the country. Clerics from the Christian, Jewish, and Muslim faiths, the Navajo Nation, Sikhs, Mormons, Baha'i, Buddhists, and Hindus, represented their faiths, offering prayers asking for protection and wisdom for the new President and his administration.

Imam Mohamed Magid and Mr. Sajid Tarar represented the Muslim faith. Magid has been the Imam of All Dulles Area Muslim Society (ADAMS) Center in Sterling, Virginia (a member of the Safa Group) for twenty years, and was president of ISNA, one of the premier organizations founded by the

---

[273] "Council On American–Islamic Relations: Its Use Of Lawfare and Intimidation" by Deborah Weiss. Front Page Magazine, August 28, 2014.
http://www.frontpagemag.com/fpm/239645/council-american–islamic-relations-its-use-lawfare-deborah-weiss

Muslim Brotherhood, from 2010 to 2014. His current website is associated with isna.net. [274]

In January 2017, Faith Leaders for America (FLA) issued a strong statement opposing Imam Mohamed Magid's inclusion in the service, calling him a senior Muslim Brotherhood leader in America and "a particularly effective practitioner of the Muslim Brotherhood's "civilization jihad."[275] Their concerns were dismissed and Magid did indeed represent his Muslim faith at the service.

There were, in fact, good reasons for opposing Magid's participation. In March 2002, the offices of the All Dulles Area Muslim Society (ADAMS) Center, which he headed, were raided by U.S. Customs authorities. Customs Agent David Kane testified that Majid's mosque was being used to launder hundreds of thousands of dollars for the targeted terror finance network that shared offices with ADAMS. Eleven ADAMS Center officials were named as targets of their terror finance investigation.[276]

In 2005, Magid was asked to give an interview to Time Magazine as a representative imam in the U.S. In the resulting article by Douglas Waller Sterling, the author wrote, "Magid regularly tips off the bureau [FBI]," a statement which Magid felt compelled to deny this in an open letter to the entire ADAMS community, saying, "the purpose of the meetings [with the FBI] are solely to create avenues to work with law enforcement to preserve our civil liberties and civil rights," he wrote.[277]

Sajid Tarar is not an imam. He calls himself a "Muslim for Trump" and supported the President during his campaign. For his support and loyalty, he was asked to give the closing benediction at the Republican Convention in 2016. He opened with a statement, "Let's pray to get our country back . . . . The values reflected by our leader must reflect the values of our

---

[274] Magid headed the Islamic Society of North America (ISNA). ISNA is a Muslim Brotherhood organization, cited as an unindicted co-conspirator in the Holy Land trial for supporting Hamas and showing its ties to other Brotherhood organizations. Its conferences in the U.S. draw thousands of Muslims each year. In 2010, Magid was named to President Obama's Department of Homeland Security (DHS) "Countering Violent Extremism Working Group, and was a strong proponent of erasing from its Countering Violent Extremism" curriculum any suggestion that Muslim terrorism draws its inspiration from the laws and doctrines of Islam. ("Jihadis in Suits Infiltrate Trump's National Prayer Service" by Clare Lopez. CNS News, January 25, 2017. https://counterjihadreport.com/tag/imam-mohamed-magid/)

[275] "Faith Leaders For America Denounce Imam Mohamed Magid; Call On President Trump To Designate Magid's Terrorist Muslim Brotherhood"

[276] "Blind to Terror: Gov't's Disastrous Muslim Outreach Efforts" by Patrick Poole. Middle East Review of International Affairs, Vol. 17, No. 2 (Summer 2013, , May 12, 2015. http://unconstrainedanalytics.org/blind-to-terror-govts-disastrous-muslim-outreach-efforts/

[277] "An American Imam," by Douglas Wallace Sterling. *Time*, November 14, 2005, http://www.time.com/time/magazine/article/0,9171,1129587,00.html;http://www.adamsce nter.org/Content.asp?ID=226

forefathers."[278] He was later asked to offer a prayer at the inauguration prayer service, as well. What was unique and troubling this time was that he recited the Surah al-Fatiha ("The Opening), the first and shortest verse in the Quran. These verses are also probably the most repeated in the Quran because they are a part of every prayer cycle in the daily worship of Muslims. That this prayer was chosen by Tarar as appropriate for this interfaith service, recited as it was in Arabic, must be considered significant, because it is insulting to both the Christians and the Jews in the cathedral that day and to the larger audience who viewed it electronically.

Tarar did not translate his prayer into English. In this interfaith context, it could only have been recited in its original Arabic, because its last line asserts the superiority of Islam among world religions, and tells the believing Muslim to reject the 'way' of the Jew, who is despised by Allah, and the Christian, who has strayed from Allah's teachings. The last two verses are translated in the Noble Quran as follows:

6. Guide us to the Straight Way,

*7. The Way of those on whom You have bestowed Your Grace, not
(the way) of those who earned Your Anger [such as the Jews], nor
of those who went astray [such as the Christians].[279]*

As explained in the annotations (in brackets), just as they appear in the Noble Quran, the terms "those who have earned your anger" refers to the Jews, of whom Mohammed said, "those whom Allah has cursed and with whom He became angry and made of them apes and pigs and slaves of Taghut."[280]

Likewise, "nor of those who went astray" refers to Christians. Scholar of Islam, the Reverend Mark Durie wrote, "...that Christians have gone astray and Jews are objects of divine wrath, must be considered a matter of central importance for interfaith relations. This is all the more so because the interpretation of verse 7 which relates it to Christians and Jews is soundly based upon the words of Muhammad himself. As Surah al-Fatihah represents the core beliefs of Islam itself, the meaning of these words cannot be ignored or glossed over."[281]

---

[278] "Meet the Muslim guy who took the convention stage and prayed for Trump" by Abigail Houslohner. Washington Post, July 19, 2016. https://www.washingtonpost.com/news/post-politics/wp/2016/07/19/meet-the-muslim-with-an-unusual-record-praying-in-arabic-at-the-rnc-tonight/?utm_term=.c0ffeb5dea26

[279] Translation from the Noble Quran, published by Dar Us-Salam.
http://www.noblequran.com/translation/index.html

[280] Quran, Noble Quran. https://quran.com/5/59-60 The word *Taghut* means to "cross the limits, overstep boundaries," or "to rebel." In Islamic theology, the word refers to idolatry.

[281] "The Greatest Recitation Of Surat Al-Fatihah" by Mark Durie. December 3, 2009.
http://blog.markdurie.com/2009/12/greatest-recitation-of-surat-al-fatiha.html

And herein lies the deception that characterizes the so-called interfaith programs, which have been growing so popular in America since 9/11, and underscores their greatest flaw. The basic belief that pervades these programs is that Jews, Christians, and Muslims all pray to one God, giving logic to the argument that we should be able to find common ground for living together in peace. But observant Muslims, whose understanding of the Quran is literal (as is obligatory), do not believe this. In the Quran, Allah curses the Jews and Christians[282], and forbids Muslims to be friends with them[283]. Observant Muslims believe that their God, *Allah* in Arabic, is greater than the God (or gods) worshipped by non-Muslims, and the statement "Allahu Akhbar" or "Allah is greater" is often used as a jihad war cry.

Thus the efforts of well-meaning and naïve Christians and Jews, who reach out to religious Muslims in an effort to 'build bridges' within the ecumenical community, too often open the doors to the underlying mission of Hamas, CAIR, and the Muslim Brotherhood, to infiltrate and undermine those who reject Islam as their religion and Allah as their God. Comfortable practicing *taqiyyah*[284] in order to further their greater mission, they pursue their goal to participate in the "grand Jihad in eliminating and destroying the Western civilization from within and 'sabotaging' its miserable house by their hands and the hands of the believers so that it is eliminated and Allah's religion is made victorious over all other religions."[285]

So when jihadist organizations call for interfaith outreach and participate in interfaith programs, there is legitimate room for concern. There is the very real apprehension that a hidden agenda, consistent with the ideological mission of Islamic resurgence and ultimate dominance, is at play. No doubt there are some Muslims who sincerely believe in outreach to their non-Muslim neighbors. But the duplicity of those engaged in civilization jihad puts all Muslims under a cloud of suspicion that such outreach may be tainted.

---

[282] For example: Surah Hud (Prophet Hood) 11:17 "...but those of the sects (Jews, Christians and all the other non-Muslim nations) that reject it (the Qur'an), the Fire will be their promised meeting-place. So be not in doubt about it (i.e. those who denied Prophet Muhammad and also denied all that which he brought from Allah, surely, they will enter Hell). Translation from the Noble Quran. http://dar-us-salam.com/TheNobleQuran/surah11.html

[283] For example: Surah Al-Ma'idah (The Table Spread with Food) 5:51. "O you who believe! Take not the Jews and the Christians as *Auliya'* (friends, protectors, helpers, etc.), they are but *Auliya'* to one another. And if any amongst you takes them as *Auliya'*, then surely he is one of them." Translation from the Noble Quran. http://dar-us-salam.com/TheNobleQuran/surah5.html

[284] Taqiyyah is the Arabic term that means "dissimulation" and is translated loosely to mean "lying for the sake of Islam"

[285] Quoted from "An Explanatory Memorandum"

Jihad by Lawfare

Lawfare is a form of asymmetric warfare in a civilian context. It uses the legal system against an enemy, real or perceived, and constitutes the abuse of the legal and judicial systems to achieve strategic goals – specifically, to silence anyone who presents opposition to their mission. In recent years, CAIR has used the American legal system in every way possible to challenge those it considers have offended it, or Islam, or Muslims in any situation. The Lawfare Project[286] defines "lawfare" as the ""abuse of Western laws and judicial systems to achieve strategic military or political ends."[287] In the case of the Muslim Brotherhood and its proxies, lawfare is used to silence the opposition, and to further its own agenda. In 2008, the United Nations reported that lawfare "has served to discourage critical media reporting on matters of serious public interest."[288]

CAIR uses U.S. law to further its Islamic agenda. It wages battles against its perceived adversaries by using the law as a weapon. CAIR's website at www.Cair.com and its daily newsletters are filled with articles about new grievances and lawsuits against those it accuses of bias and "Islamophobia."

Using the legal system to file countless, often frivolous, complaints and lawsuits as forms of extortion and intimidation, CAIR employs lawfare for the purpose of silencing its critics and furthering its jihadi program for America. In its suits, CAIR frequently carries the process right up to discovery, at which point, when it feels it cannot go further without compromising its mission or revealing its secrets, it typically withdraws its suit or agrees to settle, and closes the book on further revealing its agenda. CAIR uses a campaign of lawfare to enhance its public relations program as much as a remedy to right perceived wrongs.

The ongoing program of CAIR -sponsored lawsuits is seemingly endless. On February 10, 2017, CAIR addressed the growing movement in the U.S. to promote ALAC (American Law for American Courts), state-level legislation that would prohibit the application of foreign laws in U.S. courts to supersede American law. CAIR announced that it had sent letters to elected representatives in the state legislatures of Idaho, Arkansas, Oregon, and Montana specifically demanding that they oppose "unconstitutional, anti-Muslim legislation prohibiting state courts from considering so-called 'foreign laws.[289] In this way, CAIR was pre-empting legislative process by

---

[286] www.thelawfareproject.org

[287] "CAIR Intimidates Opponents With New Tactic: 'Lawfare'" by Ryan Mauro. The Clarion Project. http://www.clarionproject.org/analysis/new-study-documents-cairs-latest-tactic-lawfare

[288] Ibid.

putting pressure on state legislators *before* they were to address the question of applying 'foreign laws' in place of U.S. law.

ALAC was originally formulated to protect the Constitutional rights of American citizens against the imposition of *any* foreign laws or legal doctrine in American courts, although there was particular concern about the imposition of shariah. CAIR leaders have emphasized the scope of the national campaign against this proposed law, which they said was "designed to attack the religious principles of Islam, or 'shariah.'" At the time of publication, ten states prohibit the use of foreign law in their state courts in cases where Americans would be disadvantaged by not prioritizing U.S. law.[290] Fifteen additional states have introduced legislation to address the issue. Although CAIR insists that ALAC is an attack on shariah specifically and Muslims in general, Clare Lopez has clearly articulated the purpose of the law:

"There's a real misconception out there about these ALAC & ALAC-type bills – ALAC stands for 'American Laws for American Courts' – it doesn't ban any law outright, not French law or Chinese law or Singaporean law or shariah – it says if ever there's a conflict in US Courts w/US Constitutional law, then American law will prevail. Very common sense, totally inoffensive to anyone."[291]

It should be obvious that in U.S. courts, the laws of United States should supersede foreign laws. When such laws come into conflict, American law should take precedence. ALAC This has been true for every religious group in America. There are, for example, Rabbinical courts that act to pass judgment on specific kinds of Jewish law, such as religious marriage and divorce, but the religious law is always consistent with American law, and when they come into conflict, which is rare, American law trumps Jewish religious law. Not so with shariah. On a wide range of religious issues, including laws on marriage and divorce, marital rape, honor killings, and a host of other issues, shariah-supremacists want shariah to prevail, even when, as in these cases, shariah is in direct opposition to American law, and Islamic court rulings are plainly illegal. ALAC laws have already passed in as it is applied in North Carolina, Alabama, Arizona, Kansas, Louisiana, South Dakota, and Tennessee.

By waging 'lawfare' against those it perceives to be its enemies, shariah-supremacists, championed by CAIR, further their underlying mission to stifle criticism of Islam, deter future critics, and advance the

---

[290] The law, known as ALAC (American Laws for American Courts), has already been adopted in Alabama, Arkansas, Arizona, Louisiana, Kansas, Mississippi, North Carolina, Oklahoma, South Dakota and Tennessee. http://www.ncsl.org/research/civil-and-criminal-justice/2017-legislation-regarding-the-application-of-foreign-law-by-state-courts.aspx

[291] "Montana Democrats Vote Against Bill Banning Shariah Law, Call It 'Repugnant'" Breitbart, March 31, 2017. Reprinted by Counter Jihad Report, April 2, 2017. https://counterjihadreport.com/tag/alac/

status of Islam in the United States. In a study by Citizens for National Security[292], nearly 150 cases have been cataloged in which CAIR used "lawfare" techniques to intimidate and discourage its opponents. This includes the promotion of shariah as a substitute for U.S. law, a major goal of the Hamas/CAIR/Muslim Brotherhood agenda. Through the use of lawfare, CAIR protects its primary and secondary mission of supporting Hamas terrorism against Israel and promoting the Islamization of America.

Jihad by Medifare

A rarely-mentioned place where Islam has entered into an area of American life with the intention of changing the culture has made the practice of medicine more difficult and dangerous. Carol Brown has documented[293] areas where Islamic adherence to shariah in hospital settings has brought risk into patient care and reintroduced the danger of infection in areas that were thought to have been abolished more than a century ago. They include "Muslim health care workers refusing to uphold infection control protocols, Muslim medical students refusing to study topics they deem forbidden according to Islamic law, Muslim visitors in hospitals ignoring hygiene guidelines to protect patients, and hospitals bending over backwards ... to accommodate Muslim demands above and beyond anything done for members of any other religious or demographic group" (such as requiring Muslim prayer rooms, halal food, and the construction of ritual foot baths).

They also include Muslim doctors and nurses who won't use the ubiquitous antiseptic hand cleaners because they contain alcohol, and female practitioners who insist on wearing long sleeves for modesty, although this can increase the risk of transferring bacteria and other pathogens from one patient to another.

Another area of health care concerns lies in the tens of thousands of 'refugees' who have been brought to America from Muslim countries but were inadequately screened for communicable diseases. American hospitals have already seen outbreaks of diseases that have been gone from the U.S. for decades. People who have entered the U.S. illegally without medical screening have brought a resurgence of whooping cough, mumps, measles, scarlet fever, tuberculosis, small pox, and even plague and leprosy. This is all the more dangerous because Americans have lost their immunity to many of these diseases and supplies of vaccines have long since been

---

[292] "Council on American-Islamic Relations: Its Use of Lawfare and Intimidation" by Citizens for National Security.

[293] "Creeping Shariah in Health Care" by Carol Brown. *American Thinker*, July 28, 2016 http://www.americanthinker.com/articles/2016/07/creeping_shariah_in_health_care_.html#i xzz4WXtUe85U

depleted. This phenomenon has already been seen as a result of the massive influx in recent years of illegal immigrants from South America.

The combination of inadequate attention to infection control protocols among shariah-adherent Muslim health care professionals, and the re-introduction of diseases for which there is insufficient protection spells a potentially catastrophic situation in America's health care system. This little discussed area of concern may soon become significantly more relevant as small clusters of disease begin to appear across the country, and may once again threaten to become epidemic in proportion.

Jihad by Edufare

In 2005, President George Bush initiated a program to introduce into the public school system a detailed, ten lesson program, designed to be used in grades 5 through 12, called "Access Islam." The program, which was developed by the U.S. Department of Education and expanded under the Obama administration, is a detailed, hands-on study program about Islam, its customs and prayers, and a sanitized version of its ideology. "Access Islam" is supported by federal funds and promoted and distributed by the National Public Broadcasting Service and Ohio State University, which both operate multiple websites on which they post the detailed lesson plans and teachers notes.[294]

The lesson plans include worksheets and videos to help students not only learn about Islam, but perform the proclamation of Muslim faith and learn the 5 Pillars of Islam, including prayer, fasting, and *zakat* (or obligatory annual tax payment) . The fifth pillar, pilgrimage to Mecca, is the only one the children are, of course, not required to execute in this program. Through this program, however, the children learn how to perform a Muslim prayer, memorize verses from the Quran, dress in traditional Muslim clothing, learn the importance of the zakat tax (minus its obligatory use for jihad), and even try fasting to emulate the Muslim practice of abstaining from food and water from dawn to dusk during Ramadan.

On June 25, 1962, the U.S. Supreme Court ruled that the prayer, "Almighty God, we acknowledge our dependence upon Thee, and we beg Thy blessings upon us, our parents, our teachers and our Country," when uttered in a public school setting, was contrary to U.S. Constitution because it violated their First Amendment rights, which prevented the government from establishing and promoting religion. In 1963, the court also banned Bible reading in school.

According to Dennis Michael Lynch, the Christian Action Network (CAN) "has retained the law firm of Carroll, Ucker and Hemmer, LLC and they have contacted Secretary of Education Betsy DeVos, as well as Paula

---

[294] See: http://www.thirteen.org/edonline/accessislam/lesson.html

Kerger (Public Broadcasting Service) and Michael Drake (Ohio State University), demanding that the "Access Islam" program be terminated because it is in violation of the Establishment Clause of the First Amendment, which prohibits the use of public monies to promote religion."[295]

The Supreme Court rulings raise serious questions about how children can be forbidden to pray in school, even silent prayer, but a large 'educational' unit on Islam, which includes prayer, can be allowed. It speaks to the extraordinary success and the degree of influence that the Muslim Brotherhood has achieved in bringing Islam into the public schools – with government endorsement and funding – under the guise of 'education'.

Hijra – Jihad Disguised as 'Refugee Resettlement'

There is increasing evidence of CAIR's involvement in actively promoting *hijra* (Muslim migration) to the United States through its active support of America's national resettlement program, encouraging the importation of 'refugees' from countries all over the world, particularly from countries rife with terrorism. In her blog on refugee resettlement, Ann Corcoran wrote, "We have long suspected that they [CAIR] have been quietly advancing the *hijra* to America, but again, only recently have we seen news that they are out in the open promoting refugee resettlement."[296] Dr. Ibrahim B. Syed defines *hijra* as "the transition from a position where Muslims represented a small group of people, surrounded by enemies and threatened by death, to the position of a regional power with a strong central leadership. This was one that was surrounded by a large number of followers and allies." He further explains that *hijra* is the "Transition from being a simple Islamic group of believers, to being the Islamic nation. This was an organized Islamic state, with a central leadership and other organizations."[297]

The massive flow of Muslim immigrants to Europe, which began first as workers and then as a flood of refugees, has already heavily impacted life in Europe and threatened the traditions that shaped Europe over many centuries. In Germany alone, the rate of crimes committed by refugees, asylum-seekers, and illegal immigrants in 2016 rose by 52.7% over the

---

[295] "'Access Islam' curriculum in public schools exposed" by Dennis Michael Lynch, March 31, 2017. http://dennismichaellynch.com/access-islam-curriculum-public-schools-exposed/

[296] "CAIR steps into refugee debate in Redlands, CA" Posted by Ann Corcoran, October 15, 2015. https://refugeeresettlementwatch.wordpress.com/2015/10/15/cair-steps-into-refugee-debate-in-redlands-ca/

[297] "The Significance of the Hijrah", by Dr. Ibrahim B. Syed. https://historyofislam.com/contents/the-age-of-faith/the-significance-of-the-hijrah-622-ce/

previous year. 174,438 crimes were committed by immigrants under Angela Merkel's 2016 "open-door" refugee policy.[298]

The migration in the U.S. began slowly, however, until the Obama years, when the numbers exploded. The Refugee Resettlement Program in the United States is organized by the State Department and implemented by nine major voluntary international religious and immigration aid groups that serve as paid federal contractors, and hundreds of subcontractors. These groups represent a mosaic of American diversity, but are carrying out a policy in the name of 'humanitarianism' that is both foolhardy and dangerous. The nine key organizations are: the Church World Service (CWS), the Ethiopian Community Development Council (ECDC), Episcopal Migration Ministries (EMM), Hebrew Immigrant Aid Society (HIAS), International Rescue Committee (IRC) (secular), US Committee for Refugees and Immigrants (USCRI) (secular), the Lutheran Immigration and Refugee Services (LIRS), the United States Conference of Catholic Bishops (USCCB), and the World Relief Corporation (WR). [299] These nine agencies "monopolize federal grants and contracts for placing refugees in 180 (and counting) cities across America."[300]

Between October 1, 2016 through January 31, 2017, 32,475 refugees arrived in the United States, and were bundled off to their new homes in such remote places as Maine, Montana, and Arkansas, as well as Texas, California, and New York. In the first ten months of 2016, 13,210 Syrian refugees came into the United States, of whom 99.1 percent were Muslims and 0.5 percent were Christians, although it has been the Christians who were particularly and horribly targeted in Syria. Only 0.18 percent of the embattled Yazidis were included in this resettlement program.[301] While it has been argued that UNHRC only selects refugees for resettlement from its own refugee camps, and the vast majority of refugees in the camps are Sunni Muslims, according to data from the Refugee Processing Center,[302] 491,000 Syrian Christian refugees, or 11% of the 4.4 million Christian refugees from Syria, were living in UNHCR camps as of January 2017.

---

[298] "Migrant crime in Germany rises by 50 per cent, new figures show" by Justsin Huggler. The Telegraph, April 25, 2017. http://www.telegraph.co.uk/news/2017/04/25/migrant-crime-germany-rises-50-per-cent-new-figures-show/

[299] *Refugee Resettlement And The Hijra To America*, by Anne Corcoran. Center for Security Policy, 2015. https://www.centerforsecuritypolicy.org/wp-content/uploads/2015/04/Refugee_Resettlement_Hijra.pdf

[300] Ibid

[301] "13,210 Syrian Refugees So Far in 2016; Up 675% from 2015; 99.1% Are Muslims" by Patrick Goodenough. CNSNews.com, November 1, 2016. http://www.cnsnews.com/news/article/patrick-goodenough/13210-syrian-refugees-admitted-year-through-october-675-99-are

[302] http://ireports.wrapsnet.org

The flow of 'refugees' into the United States continues, although a Supreme Court ruling in June 2017, regarding President Donald Trump's Executive Order No. 13780, "Protecting the Nation From Foreign Terrorist Entry Into the United States," allowed the government to limit immigration from six predominantly Muslim countries.

Executive Order No. 13780 also reduced the ceiling of refugee admissions from 110,000 for FY 2017 to 50,000, suspended the refugee resettlement program for 120 days, enabled enhance vetting procedures for refugee admission, and granted state and local jurisdictions a role in the process of determining refugee placement in their jurisdictions. Between October 1, 2016 and April 30, 2017, 42,414 refugees were admitted into the U.S.[303]

Jihad in the Mosques: Hate Speech from the Pulpit

The 2016 elections was witness to an unleashing of hateful rhetoric and street violence that has changed the landscape in America. Not limited to Black Lives Matter followers shouting "What do we want? Dead Cops! When do we want it? Now!," this growing loss of inhibition and lack of common decency has found its way onto college campuses, where pro-Hamas and BDS demonstrations have led to violence, and into the pulpits of some mosques throughout the country, where imams incite hatred and violence.

In his Friday sermon on July 21, 2017, at the Islamic Center of Riverside, California, Sheikh Mahmoud Harmoush delivered a sermon in which he prayed, "Oh Allah, liberate the Al-Aqsa Mosque and all the Muslim lands from the unjust tyrants and the occupiers [Israelis]. Oh Allah, destroy them, they are no match for You. Oh Allah, disperse them, and rend them asunder. Turn them into booty [slaves] in the hands of the Muslims. ... Allah wants us to have jihad in our lives, no matter what and where we are," he said.[304, 305]

Ammar Shahin, imam of the Islamic Center at Davis, California, used his Friday sermon to call on Allah to "liberate the al-Aqsa Mosque from the

---

[303] "Refugees and Asylees in the United States" By Jie Zong and Jeanne Batalova. Migration Policy Institute, June 7, 2017. http://www.migrationpolicy.org/article/refugees-and-asylees-united-states

[304] "California: Imam at San Bernardino Jihadist's Mosque Calls Muslims...to Jihad" Creeping Shariah, July 28, 2017 https://creepingshariah.wordpress.com/2017/07/28/cali-imam-jihad/

[305] "California Imam Mahmoud Harmoush Prays for Allah to Destroy the Jews: They Are After Mecca and Medina" Memri-TV, July 21, 2017. https://www.memri.org/tv/california-sermon-jews-plotting-mecca-medina-allah-wants-jihad/transcript

filth of the Jews .... count them one by one and annihilate them down to the very last one. Do not spare any of them."[306]

Civilization Jihad in America

Dutch Parliamentarian Geert Wilders, who has been under assault in his own country for his outspoken views on the Muslim *hijra* in Europe, wrote:

> *"... [O]ne can see that the threat from Islam doesn't just come in the form of Islamic terrorism by suicide bombers trying to wreak havoc in our cities. More often, it comes in the form of gradual and incremental transformation of our societies and legal systems, or what is termed 'Islamization' of our democratic societies by the vast growing numbers of Muslim immigrants who are importing Islam into our Western way of life."* [307]

The variety of tactics that have been employed in the United States by the Muslim Brotherhood and its vast stable of proxies has achieved a great deal over the last 25 years or so. The establishment of CAIR as the legitimate advocate for all Muslims in the U.S., the inclusion of influential Muslims in high places (particularly Muslims who have been associated with Muslim Brotherhood-linked groups), the widespread social acceptance of Muslim demands for an increasing number of Muslim religious requirements (including the construction of footbaths, prayer rooms, the provision of prayer time during the work or school day, halal food, and special working conditions), is proof positive that the Muslim Brotherhood's strategic plan, as spelled out in the Explanatory Memorandum, has already achieved much, all in the name of diversity and inclusion.

The Brotherhood's hidden agenda has largely escaped the American public that embraces these concepts. The threat is that civilization jihad is a Trojan Horse, carrying within it the seeds of destruction to the American way of life as it promotes Islam and shariah at the expense of liberty and personal choice.

Hamas as a Threat to American National Security

In the early morning of November 9, 2016, barely minutes after the election of Donald Trump to the U.S. Presidency was announced, the

---

[306] foxnews.com/opinion/2017/07/28/now-s-sorry-california-imam-preaches-sound-bites-hate.html

[307] Modern Day Trojan Horse: Al-Hijra, the Islamic Doctrine of Immigration, Accepting Freedom or Imposing Islam?" by Sam Solomon and E. Al-Maqdisi.
https://centurean2.wordpress.com/2011/04/02/sam-solomons-al-hijra-the-islamic-doctrine-of-immigration-modern-day-trojan-horse/

Executive Director of CAIR's Los Angeles branch, Hussam Ayloush, brought the threat of jihad in the U.S. clearly into focus. Ayloush tweeted a phrase usually associated with the so-called 'Arab Spring'. He wrote:

> "Ok, repeat after me: *Al-Shaab yureed isqat al-nizaam.* The people want to bring down the regime."[308]

While it could be argued that the tweet was one of thousands of others reflecting the anger and frustration over a stunning political loss by the Democrats, and that Ayloush quickly walked it back, it nevertheless reflects the deeply embedded belief among Muslim Brotherhood followers that one of its prime underlying aims is making Islamic law the predominant legal system in America. Ayloush, the director of a prominent chapter of CAIR, was calling - directly and without artifice - for the overthrow of the U.S. government.

Despite statements like this by people like Ayloush, many Americans still favor the progressive concept that promotes diversity and tolerance over all. They mock and curse those who expose the creeping influence of jihad and shariah in our society, branding them "Islamophobes". Because of such attitudes, the freedoms, which once defined us, have now been turned against us. Universities have become hotbeds of political correctness run amok, where the freedoms of speech and assembly have become a right for radicals only, and are forbidden to those with whom they disagree. Our prisons have become breeding grounds for indoctrinating inmates with the tenets of Islam. Even our military has become a nurturing environment for those who proselytize for Islam.

People who have been linked to Hamas-supporting organizations now run for public office and have been both elected and appointed to important positions in local, state, and federal government. The freedom with which the Hamas/CAIR/Muslim Brotherhood nexus has been able to gain and keep its American program active and productive is at once astonishing and shameful.

It is difficult for Western intelligence analysts and law enforcement professionals to even recognize, much less understand, the intricacies of the jihadi mindset that drive those who support Islamic terrorism. Because fundraising for Hamas – directly and indirectly – is illegal, and recruitment of supporters for jihad, as they practice it, lies in gray, poorly defined layers of local, state, and federal law, the deviously-orchestrated secret operations that Hamas supporters employ to hide their activities have been extraordinarily successful. They both hide and display their ideology. By concealing it from authorities and displaying it to their followers, they present a bewildering array of messages that are difficult for law enforcement to comprehend. They are therefore too often overlooked and ignored.

Americans are traditionally generous and tolerant, overlooking differences between people and their beliefs and lifestyles in favor of

---

[308] Arab Spring chant posted on Twitter.com, November 9, 2016.

welcoming the diversity that has historically characterized life in America. But what is too often disregarded by many Americans in the twenty-first century, blinded by the concept of 'diversity' and 'multiculturalism', is that the practice and support of civilization jihad in any and all of its manifestations and the adherence to shariah in contravention of U.S. law is antithetical to the American Constitution and to American values and tradition.

Hamas is a classic example of an ideology that despises the freedoms that Americans cherish. Instead, it embraces shariah and imposes it harshly in areas under its control, such as Gaza. And the individuals and organizations that support this concept are enemies of the nation which gives them the right to practice their beliefs.

The 'nonviolence' and 'peace-loving' characterization of the Muslim Brotherhood is a myth. Those in the U.S. who support and protect Hamas also hold shariah as an essential part of their core ideology, even when their public faces appear to fit into the American way of life. The Hamas/CAIR/Muslim Brotherhood nexus is most dangerous when it is ignored by a well-meaning but naïve and ill-informed American public.

Left alone to fulfill its mission, this triple threat intends to make Islamic law supreme in the United States and turn America into an Islamic nation governed under shariah. The Muslim Brotherhood has said many times that this is its plan, and has already made enormous strides in its efforts to make Islam dominant in America. America should be listening.

Jihadis consistently use the very institutions against America that have made this country unique in the world. While pretending to be a part of the system, they work diligently to destroy it from within, as they promised they would. The translation of the word "Islam" is "submission",[309] submission to Allah, the Arabic word for God. Contrary to the loyalty and patriotism expressed on some of their English language websites, the doctrine of Islam requires that they reject personal freedom, and demands allegiance to shariah and the commands of the Quran.

Islam teaches that only Islam is the one true faith, and the only path that leads to salvation.[310] While it is not the only major religion to hold such views, it is the only one that allows and even encourages the use of violence to further its reach and defeat non-believers. To the jihadis who constitute the core of the Hamas/CAIR/Muslim Brotherhood nexus, their belief system is anathema to American values. While they consider our love of liberty and personal responsibility evil, their own Islamic law countenances honor killings, female genital mutilation, stoning, the amputation of hands and

---

[309] "An Introduction to Islam through Questions and Answers" IslamCan.com http://www.islamcan.com/islamic-articles/an-introduction-to-islam-through-questions-and-answers.shtml

[310] "The World's Muslims: Religion, Politics and Society", Chapter 6: Interfaith Relations Pew Research Center, April 30, 2013 http://www.pewforum.org/2013/04/30/the-worlds-muslims-religion-politics-society-interfaith-relations/

feet, and extra-judicial execution as legitimate parts of its legal system. Moreover, classic Islam not only claims to be the only path to paradise, it considers all other religions, particularly the Jewish and Christian faiths, to be subservient to them, and can find in the Quran justification for taxing, enslaving them, and killing them.

Their mission to destroy American Constitutional law and replace it with shariah is fundamental. In 1934, Hassan al-Banna, who founded the Muslim Brotherhood in 1928, wrote, "It is a duty incumbent on every Muslim to struggle towards the aim of making every people Muslim and the whole world Islamic, so that the banner of Islam can flutter over the earth and the call of the Muezzin can resound in all the corners of the world: God is greatest [Allahu akbar]!"[311]

Civilization jihad is a stealth jihad. Increasingly, supporters of the Hamas/CAIR/Muslim Brotherhood nexus demand more accommodation to their religion and public access to their religious needs, as mentioned earlier. This included their own shariah courts, the right, and sometimes a requirement, for women to dress 'modestly' (which may mean completely covering her face and thus masking her identity), the right to take multiple prayer breaks at work, the requirement of providing 'halal' food at schools and in office cafeterias, the recognition of Muslim religious holidays in public schools, and finally, the application of Islamic law to pre-empt U.S. law.

Slowly but steadily, they have been succeeding,. Muslim taxi drivers refuse to take passengers carrying alcohol, or traveling with service dogs, which they consider unclean. Cashiers refuse to check out customers who have purchased liquor or pork. Foot washing stations and prayer rooms in public universities and airports have become increasingly common, although similar accommodations are not made for other faiths. These are small but meaningful steps in their civilization jihad. If they can continue to accomplish them, as Abdurahman Alamoudi said, and many others have echoed, "This will be a Muslim country".

In reality, they still have a long way to go. Muslims represent a tiny part of America's population. Pew Research Center has reported[312] that some 3.3 million Muslims lived in the U.S. at the end of 2015. This represents slightly more than 1% of the country's population. The support system they have built around their community and the people who fight on their behalf in the name of 'diversity' and 'humanity', while also small in size, are nevertheless extremely vocal and activist. Their alliances with other activist groups like BDS, bring them publicity, giving them both

---

[311] *The Society of the Muslim Brothers in Egypt,* by Brynjar Lia. Ithaca Press, 1998. P. 28.

[312] "A new estimate of the U.S. Muslim population" by Besheer Mohamed. Pew Research Center, January 6, 2016. http://www.pewresearch.org/fact-tank/2016/01/06/a-new-estimate-of-the-u-s-muslim-population/

strength and a national platform, which helps them spread their message, recruit followers, and push forward in their mission.

They fervently believe that they can accomplish their goal. The riots in Berkley and New York, the raging war against American police, the ferocious movement to bring down America's newly-elected president, these are all evidence that America can, in fact, be fundamentally changed from what it was meant to be. It does not matter whether or not we believe they can succeed. *They* believe it and so they will use every means at their disposal to try to accomplish it.

The unholy collaboration of Hamas, CAIR, and the Muslim Brotherhood will continue its work to support Hamas' murderous fight against Israel in every way it can. It will also continue to expand its plans to carry out civilization jihad in the United States by infiltrating and undermining our institutions in every area of our lives.

The terrorist organization that finds its women and children expendable in Gaza, and that in its founding document identifies Jews everywhere as an enemy that must be destroyed, is the same organization that operates in the U.S. under the protection of CAIR and the elusive, secretive, but powerful Muslim Brotherhood. Hamas' mission here, beyond supporting its operations in the Middle East, is to subvert the United States government, create from it a new Islamic state governed under shariah, and replace the Constitution with Islamic Law. The inroads that the Hamas/CAIR/Muslim Brotherhood nexus has already made in its program to infiltrate all of American society – in our schools, in our communities, in our government, and in our future – are significant and will continue to advance in the face of an uninformed America.

The record goes all the way back to the 1980s. A declassified FBI report reveals the Muslim Brotherhood's activities in the United States at the time:

> *"(CI) has advised that the Ikhwan is a secret Muslim organization that has unlimited funds and is extremely well organized in the United States to the point where it has set up political action front groups with no traceable ties to the IIIT[313] or its various Muslim groups. They also have claimed success in infiltrating the United States government...the IIIT leadership has indicated that in this phase their organization needs to peacefully get inside the United States Government and also American universities. (CI) noted*

---

[313] The International Institute of Islamic Thought (IIIT) describes itself as "a private, non-profit, academic, cultural and educational institution, concerned with general issues of Islamic thought and education". Its slogan is "Towards Islamization of Knowledge and Reform of Islamic Thought. The IIIT was founded at a meeting in Lugano, Switzerland, attended by Muslim Brotherhood leaders, including Youssef Qaradawi. The IIIT was founded in the U.S. in 1980 by the Muslim Brotherhood's American branch."
https://www.globalmbwatch.com/international-institute-of-islamic-thought/

that the ultimate goal of the Islamic Revolution is the overthrow of all non-Islamic governments."[314]

The seeds of civilization jihad have long since been sown and have taken root in many segments of our population. Our universities, local town and city councils, federal offices, even the mainstream media have taken up the mission to support those who cry out against 'Islamophobia', sparring with the shadows of free speech in uneven battles in which noise, vulgarity, and violence overpower the freedom of expression, courtesy, and honor.

Americans remain deeply divided. The left, still obsessed by the loss of the presidential election and consumed by a political correctness that makes them feel virtuous, has already welcomed tens of thousands of Middle Eastern refugees, over 99% of whom are Muslims. Disregarding the reality that Christians in the war-torn Middle East have been targeted with torture, sexual slavery, and death *by Muslims* in the Islamic State, Hizb'allah, Hamas, and other terrorist groups, the Obama administration and the UNHCR left them out of its 'humanitarian' program. The left, which has been clamoring for diversity, has allowed none in the flow of refugees 'rescued' from the Middle East.

One of President Trump's first efforts to stem this tide took the form of an Executive Action to temporarily stop immigration from seven jihad-dominated and failed state countries, a list that was first generated by the Obama administration. Although immediately challenged in court, the move was the beginning of an official effort to stem the flow of jihadis and jihad supporters into this country.

But more is needed. Never in the history of the U.S. has there been such deep division in the public discourse, the imposition of limitations on free speech, or the inability of the American people to overcome their differences. This prepares the stage for the agenda of the Muslim Brotherhood to further its program of civilization jihad which depends, in part, in the disarray of America's society and its inability to overcome its differences.

Unlike his predecessor, President Trump has recognized the threat and called it by name. What is needed next is to recognize the growing threat that it represents and already exists within America as a result of the consistent efforts of the Muslim Brotherhood in all its forms. Although its followers claim it to be 'non-violent, its mission is inherent in its own slogan, which it does not hide:

> *"Allah is our objective. The Prophet is our leader. The Qur'an is our law. Jihad is our way. Dying in the way of Allah is our highest hope. Allahu akbar!"*

---

[314] "North American Islamic Trust" August 17, 1988. From declassified document released under FOIA request by the Investigative Project.
http://www.investigativeproject.org/documents/misc/159.pdf

Muslim Brotherhood founder Hassan al-Banna made it even clearer:[315]

"It is in the nature of Islam to dominate, not to be dominated, to impose its law on all nations and to extend its power to the entire planet."[316]

The documentation supporting the Brotherhood's close ties with terrorism is indisputable, whether by acts of terrorism abroad, or by providing support for the terrorism of Hamas and others from America. The relationships among the Brotherhood, Hamas, and CAIR are equally well-documented, connecting them all to a vast and powerful global terrorist network. The web of terror-supporting organizations that the Muslim Brotherhood has created in the U.S. is strong and influential; the impact of their subversive activities throughout the fabric of American life has created a clear and present danger to the country. The violent demonstrations in the streets of American cities and on American university campuses, at schools and at public meetings, show how far the Brotherhood and its partners have come in creating the chaos they believe will lead to conquest.

On November 3, 2015, Representative Mario Diaz-Balart (R-Florida) introduced the "Muslim Brotherhood Terrorist Designation Act of 2015". It was never passed. Then, on January 10, 2017, Senator Ted Cruz (R-Texas) and Congressman Diaz-Balart introduced the "Muslim Brotherhood Terrorist Designation Act of 2017" in both chambers of Congress. The bills reopened a controversy that has yet to be resolved. The difficulty in designating the Brotherhood lies in the definition of "foreign terrorist organization" which has specified very specific characteristics, including the intent to engage in terrorism.[317] It also lies in the immense pressure being put on members of Congress by a lobby led by organizations like CAIR and the large number of highly vocal Muslim organizations around the country.

On February 11, 2017, CAIR released a statement that read, "Trump's plan to declare the Muslim Brotherhood a terror group is about going after American Muslims". CAIR's director of government affairs, Robert McCaw, broadcast an e-mail in which he said, "In pushing this designation, Islamophobic hate groups and their congressional allies are seeking to

---

[315] Muslim Brotherhood Terrorist Designation Act of 2015". 114TH CONGRESS 1ST SESSION H. R. 3892. https://www.congress.gov/114/bills/hr3892/BILLS-114hr3892ih.pdf

[316] The Muslim Brotherhood," The Investigative Project on Terrorism, http://www.investigativeproject.org/profile/173

[317] "It must be a *foreign organization.* The organization must *engage in terrorist activity*, as defined in section 212 (a)(3)(B) of the INA (8 U.S.C. §1182(a)(3)(B)),* or *terrorism*, as defined in section 140(d)(2) of the Foreign Relations Authorization Act, Fiscal Years 1988 and 1989 (22 U.S.C. § 2656f(d)(2)),** *or retain the capability and intent to engage in terrorist activity or terrorism.* The organization's terrorist activity or terrorism must threaten the security of U.S. nationals *or* the national security (national defense, foreign relations, *or* the economic interests) of the United States."

create a new era of witch hunts and religious McCarthyism where being an American Muslim and political detractor is enough to disqualify you from civic participation."

No, it is about recognizing the real threat posed by the secret agenda of the Muslim Brotherhood and its hundreds of organizations building out its plan for civilization jihad. This is the core of the Brotherhood's strategy. All attacks, real or imagined, true or false, are returned in kind with a vengeance that makes Muslims the victims, and the accuser the accused. But Robert McCaw, using rules straight from the Brotherhood playbook, muddies the waters in which Hamas, CAIR, and the Muslim Brotherhood use confusion, misdirection, and lies to build their program for the future as they see it. Their frontal assault of civilization jihad being waged against America is well under way.

America has always been a strong nation and a beacon of hope to the rest of the world. But it will take a powerful and dedicated initiative by a committed administration in Washington to reverse the creeping shariah being carried out by the Hamas/CAIR/Muslim Brotherhood nexus and the legions of organizations supporting it.

The fight against the Hamas/CAIR/Muslim Brotherhood nexus and its secret agenda to destroy America, depends on it first be recognized for what it is, called by name, and stopped. The Muslim Brotherhood agenda in the U.S., as described in detail throughout this volume is dedicated to subversion, infiltration, disinformation, lawfare, and the promotion of shariah, all in the name of civilization jihad.

Losing this war for America to the archaic and repressive ideology that is shariah is not an option. The infiltration of our government and our communities by ideologues, who cloak themselves in self-righteousness but reject American principles, constitutes a real and present danger to the future of America. The misuse of our laws and our social systems in the name of Islam is an affront to the principles that have made America great.

This book and its author will no doubt be labeled "Islamophobic" by those who hate the concept liberty for all Americans. It is not. It simply calls accountable those who would use Islam to sabotage and undermine the very foundation that has made America great and its people free.

America must remain the nation that its founders envisioned – a haven for all those seeking g freedom and a land of opportunity for people who understand and respect the Declaration of Independence and American Constitution, as a land of opportunity, not repression, for a people who are ready to do whatever is necessary to protect it and to remain free.

APPENDIX I

HAMAS COVENANT 1988

The Covenant of the Islamic Resistance Movement
18 August 1988

In The Name Of The Most Merciful Allah

"Ye are the best nation that hath been raised up unto mankind: ye command that which is just, and ye forbid that which is unjust, and ye believe in Allah. And if they who have received the scriptures had believed, it had surely been the better for them: there are believers among them, but the greater part of them are transgressors. They shall not hurt you, unless with a slight hurt; and if they fight against you, they shall turn their backs to you, and they shall not be helped. They are smitten with vileness wheresoever they are found; unless they obtain security by entering into a treaty with Allah, and a treaty with men; and they draw on themselves indignation from Allah, and they are afflicted with poverty. This they suffer, because they disbelieved the signs of Allah, and slew the prophets unjustly; this, because they were rebellious, and transgressed." (Al-Imran – verses 109-111).

Israel will exist and will continue to exist until Islam will obliterate it, just as it obliterated others before it" (The Martyr, Imam Hassan al-Banna, of blessed memory).

"The Islamic world is on fire. Each of us should pour some water, no matter how little, to extinguish whatever one can without waiting for the others." (Sheikh Amjad al-Zahawi, of blessed memory).

In The Name Of The Most Merciful Allah

Introduction

Praise be unto Allah, to whom we resort for help, and whose forgiveness, guidance and support we seek; Allah bless the Prophet and grant him salvation, his companions and supporters, and to those who carried out his message and adopted his laws – everlasting prayers and salvation as long as the earth and heaven will last. Hereafter:

O People: Out of the midst of troubles and the sea of suffering, out of the palpitations of faithful hearts and cleansed arms; out of the sense of duty, and in response to Allah's command, the call has gone out rallying people together and making them follow the ways of Allah, leading them to have determined will in order to fulfill their role in life, to overcome all obstacles, and surmount the difficulties on the way. Constant preparation has continued and so has the readiness to sacrifice life and all that is precious for the sake of Allah.

Thus it was that the nucleus (of the movement) was formed and started to pave its way through the tempestuous sea of hopes and expectations, of wishes and yearnings, of troubles and obstacles, of pain and challenges, both inside and outside.

When the idea was ripe, the seed grew and the plant struck root in the soil of reality, away from passing emotions, and hateful haste. The Islamic Resistance Movement emerged to carry out its role through striving for the sake of its Creator, its arms intertwined with those of all the fighters for the liberation of Palestine. The spirits of its fighters meet with the spirits of all the fighters who have sacrificed their lives on the soil of Palestine, ever since it was conquered by the companions of the Prophet, Allah bless him and grant him salvation, and until this day.

This Covenant of the Islamic Resistance Movement (Hamas), clarifies its picture, reveals its identity, outlines its stand, explains its aims, speaks about its hopes, and calls for its support, adoption and joining its ranks. Our struggle against the Jews is very great and very serious. It needs all sincere efforts. It is a step that inevitably should be followed by other steps. The Movement is but one squadron that should be supported by more and more squadrons from this vast Arab and Islamic world, until the enemy is vanquished and Allah's victory is realized.

Thus we see them coming on the horizon "and you shall learn about it hereafter" "Allah hath written, Verily I will prevail, and my apostles: for Allah is strong and mighty." (The Dispute – verse 21).

"Say to them, This is my way: I invite you to Allah, by an evident demonstration; both I and he who followeth me; and, praise be unto Allah! I am not an idolator." (Joseph – verse 107).

Hamas (means) *strength and bravery* **–(according to) Al-Mua'jam al-Wasit: c1.**

Definition of the Movement

Ideological Starting-Points

Article One:

The Islamic Resistance Movement: The Movement's program is Islam. From it, it draws its ideas, ways of thinking and understanding of the universe, life and man. It resorts to it for judgment in all its conduct, and it is inspired by it for guidance of its steps.

The Islamic Resistance Movement's Relation With the Muslim Brotherhood Group:

Article Two:

The Islamic Resistance Movement is one of the wings of Muslim Brotherhood in Palestine. Muslim Brotherhood Movement is a universal organization which constitutes the largest Islamic movement in modern times. It is maintained by its deep understanding, accurate comprehension and its complete embrace of all Islamic concepts of all aspects of life, culture, creed, politics, economics, education, society, justice and judgment, the spreading of Islam, education, art, information, science of the occult and conversion to Islam.

Structure and Formation

Article Three:

The basic structure of the Islamic Resistance Movement consists of Muslims who have given their allegiance to Allah whom they truly worship, - "I have created the jinn and humans only for the purpose of worshipping" – who know their duty towards themselves, their families and country. In all that, they fear Allah and raise the banner of Jihad in the face of the oppressors, so that they would rid the land and the people of their uncleanliness, vileness and evils.

"But we will oppose truth to vanity, and it shall confound the same; and behold, it shall vanish away." (Prophets – verse 18).

Article Four:

The Islamic Resistance Movement welcomes every Muslim who embraces its faith, ideology, follows its program, keeps its secrets, and wants to belong to its ranks and carry out the duty. Allah will certainly reward such one.

Time and Place Extent of the Islamic Resistance Movement:

Article Five:

Time extent of the Islamic Resistance Movement: By adopting Islam as its way of life, the Movement goes back to the time of the birth of the Islamic message, of the righteous ancestor, for Allah is its target, the Prophet is its example and the Koran is its constitution. Its extent in place is anywhere that there are Muslims who embrace Islam as their way of life everywhere in the globe. This being so, it extends to the depth of the earth and reaches out to the heaven.

"Dost thou not see how Allah putteth forth a parable; representing a good word, as a good tree, whose root is firmly fixed in the earth, and whose branches reach unto heaven; which bringeth forth its fruit in all seasons, by the will of its Lord? Allah propoundeth parables unto men, that they may be instructed." (Abraham – verses 24-25).

Characteristics and Independence:

Article Six:

The Islamic Resistance Movement is a distinguished Palestinian movement, whose allegiance is to Allah, and whose way of life is Islam. It strives to raise the banner of Allah over every inch of Palestine, for under the wing of Islam followers of all religions can coexist in security and safety where their lives, possessions and rights are concerned. In the absence of Islam, strife will be rife, oppression spreads, evil prevails and schisms and wars will break out.

How excellent was the Muslim poet, Mohamed Ikbal, when he wrote:

"If faith is lost, there is no security and there is no life for him who does not adhere to religion. He who accepts life without religion, has taken annihilation as his companion for life."

The Universality of the Islamic Resistance Movement:

Article Seven:

As a result of the fact that those Muslims who adhere to the ways of the Islamic Resistance Movement spread all over the world, rally support for it and its stands, strive towards enhancing its struggle, the Movement is a universal one. It is well-equipped for that because of the clarity of its ideology, the nobility of its aim and the loftiness of its objectives.

On this basis, the Movement should be viewed and evaluated, and its role be recognized. He who denies its right, evades supporting it and turns a blind eye to facts, whether intentionally or unintentionally, would awaken to see that events have overtaken him and with no logic to justify his attitude. One should certainly learn from past examples.

The injustice of next-of-kin is harder to bear than the smite of the Indian sword.

"We have also sent down unto thee the book of the Koran with truth, confirming that scripture which was revealed before it; and preserving the same safe from corruption. Judge therefore between them according to that which Allah hath revealed; and follow not their desires, by swerving from the truth which hath come unto thee. Unto every of you have we given a law, and an open path; and if Allah had pleased, he had surely made you one people; but he hath thought it fit to give you different laws, that he might try you in that which he hath given you respectively. Therefore strive to excel each other in good works; unto Allah shall ye all return, and then will he declare unto you that concerning which ye have disagreed." (The Table, verse 48).

The Islamic Resistance Movement is one of the links in the chain of the struggle against the Zionist invaders. It goes back to 1939, to the emergence of the martyr Izz al-Din al Kissam and his brethren the fighters, members of Muslim Brotherhood. It goes on to reach out and become one with another chain that includes the struggle of the Palestinians and Muslim Brotherhood in the 1948 war and the Jihad operations of the Muslim Brotherhood in 1968 and after.

Moreover, if the links have been distant from each other and if obstacles, placed by those who are the lackeys of Zionism in the way of the fighters obstructed the continuation of the struggle, the Islamic Resistance Movement aspires to the maintaining of Allah's promise, no matter how long that should take. The Prophet, Allah bless him and grant him salvation, has said:

"The Day of Judgment will not come about until Muslims fight the Jews (killing the Jews), when the Jew will hide behind stones and trees. The stones and trees will say O Muslims, O Abdulla, there is a Jew behind me, come and kill him. Only the Gharkad tree, would not do that because it is one of the trees of the Jews." (related by al-Bukhari and Muslim).

The Slogan of the Islamic Resistance Movement:

Article Eight:

Allah is its target, the Prophet is its model, the Koran its constitution: Jihad is its path and death for the sake of Allah is the loftiest of its wishes.

Objectives

Incentives and Objectives:

Article Nine:

The Islamic Resistance Movement found itself at a time when Islam has disappeared from life. Thus rules shook, concepts were upset, values changed and evil people took control, oppression and darkness prevailed, cowards became like tigers: homelands were usurped, people were scattered and were caused to wander all over the world, the state of justice disappeared and the state of falsehood replaced it. Nothing remained in its right place. Thus, when Islam is absent from the arena, everything changes. From this state of affairs the incentives are drawn.

As for the objectives: They are the fighting against the false, defeating it and vanquishing it so that justice could prevail, homelands be retrieved and from its mosques would the voice of the mu'azen emerge declaring the establishment of the state of Islam, so that people and things would return each to their right places and Allah is our helper.

"… and if Allah had not prevented men, the one by the other, verily the earth had been corrupted: but Allah is beneficent towards his creatures." (The Cow – verse 251).

Article Ten:

As the Islamic Resistance Movement paves its way, it will back the oppressed and support the wronged with all its might. It will spare no effort to bring about justice and defeat injustice, in word and deed, in this place and everywhere it can reach and have influence therein.

Strategies and Methods

Strategies of the Islamic Resistance Movement: Palestine Is Islamic aqf:

Article Eleven:

The Islamic Resistance Movement believes that the land of Palestine is an Islamic Waqf consecrated for future Muslim generations until Judgment Day. It, or any part of it, should not be squandered: it, or any part of it, should not be given up. Neither a single Arab country nor all Arab countries, neither any king or president, nor all the kings and presidents, neither any organization nor all of them, be they Palestinian or Arab, possess the right to do that. Palestine is an Islamic Waqf land consecrated for Muslim generations until Judgment Day. This being so, who could claim to have the right to represent Muslim generations till Judgement Day?

This is the law governing the land of Palestine in the Islamic Shariah (law) and the same goes for any land the Muslims have conquered by force, because during the times of (Islamic) conquests, the Muslims consecrated these lands to Muslim generations till the Day of Judgement.

It happened like this: When the leaders of the Islamic armies conquered Syria and Iraq, they sent to the Caliph of the Muslims, Umar bin-el-Khatab, asking for his advice concerning the conquered land – whether they should divide it among the soldiers, or leave it for its owners, or what? After consultations and discussions between the Caliph of the Muslims, Omar bin-el-Khatab and companions of the Prophet, Allah bless him and grant him salvation, it was decided that the land should be left with its owners who could benefit by its fruit. As for the real ownership of the land and the land itself, it should be consecrated for Muslim generations till Judgement Day. Those who are on the land, are there only to benefit from its fruit. This Waqf remains as long as earth and heaven remain. Any procedure in contradiction to Islamic Shariah, where Palestine is concerned, is null and void.

"Verily, this is a certain truth. Wherefore praise the name of thy Lord, the great Allah." (The Inevitable – verse 95).

Homeland and Nationalism from the Point of View of the Islamic Resistance Movement in Palestine:

Article Twelve:

Nationalism, from the point of view of the Islamic Resistance Movement, is part of the religious creed. Nothing in nationalism is more significant or deeper than in the case when an enemy should tread Muslim land. Resisting and quelling the enemy become the individual duty of every Muslim, male or female. A woman can go out to fight the enemy without her husband's permission, and so does the slave: without his master's permission.

Nothing of the sort is to be found in any other regime. This is an undisputed fact. If other nationalist movements are connected with materialistic, human or regional causes, nationalism of the Islamic Resistance Movement has all these elements as well as the more important elements that give it soul and life. It is connected to the source of spirit and the granter of life, hoisting in the sky of the homeland the heavenly banner that joins earth and heaven with a strong bond.

If Moses comes and throws his staff, both witch and magic are annulled.

"Now is the right direction manifestly distinguished from deceit: whoever therefore shall deny Tagut, and believe in Allah, he shall surely take hold with a strong handle, which shall not be broken; Allah is he who heareth and seeth." (The Cow – Verse 256).

Peaceful Solutions, Initiatives and International Conferences:

Article Thirteen:

Initiatives, and so-called peaceful solutions and international conferences, are in contradiction to the principles of the Islamic Resistance Movement. Abusing any part of Palestine is abuse directed against part of religion. Nationalism of the Islamic Resistance Movement is part of its religion. Its members have been fed on that. For the sake of hoisting the banner of Allah over their homeland they fight. "Allah will be prominent, but most people do not know."

Now and then the call goes out for the convening of an international conference to look for ways of solving the (Palestinian) question. Some accept, others reject the idea, for this or other reason, with one stipulation or more for consent to convening the conference and participating in it. Knowing the parties constituting the conference, their past and present attitudes towards Muslim problems, the Islamic Resistance Movement does not consider these conferences capable of realizing the demands, restoring the rights or doing justice to the oppressed. These conferences are only ways of setting the infidels in the land of the Muslims as arbitrators. When did the infidels do justice to the believers?

"But the Jews will not be pleased with thee, neither the Christians, until thou follow their religion; say, The direction of Allah is the true direction. And verily if thou follow their desires, after the knowledge which hath been given thee, thou shalt find no patron or protector against Allah." (The Cow – verse 120).

There is no solution for the Palestinian question except through Jihad. Initiatives, proposals and international conferences are all a waste of time and vain endeavors. The Palestinian people know better than to consent to having their future, rights and fate toyed with. As in said in the honorable Hadith:

"The people of Syria are Allah's lash in His land. He wreaks His vengeance through them against whomsoever He wishes among His slaves It is unthinkable that those who are double-faced among them should prosper over the faithful. They will certainly die out of grief and desperation."

The Three Circles:

Article Fourteen:

The question of the liberation of Palestine is bound to three circles: the Palestinian circle, the Arab circle and the Islamic circle. Each of these circles has its role in the struggle against Zionism. Each has its duties, and it is a horrible mistake and a sign of deep ignorance to overlook any of these circles. Palestine is an Islamic land which has the first of the two kiblahs (direction to which Muslims turn in praying), the third of the holy (Islamic) sanctuaries, and the point of departure for Mohamed's midnight journey to the seven heavens (i.e. Jerusalem).

"Praise be unto him who transported his servant by night, from the sacred temple of Mecca to the farther temple of Jerusalem, the circuit of which we have blessed, that we might show him some of our signs; for Allah is he who heareth, and seeth." (The Night-Journey – verse 1).

Since this is the case, liberation of Palestine is then an individual duty for very Muslim wherever he may be. On this basis, the problem should be viewed. This should be realized by every Muslim.

The day the problem is dealt with on this basis, when the three circles mobilize their capabilities, the present state of affairs will change and the day of liberation will come nearer.

"Verily ye are stronger than they, by reason of the terror cast into their breasts from Allah. This, because they are not people of prudence." (The Emigration – verse 13).

The Jihad for the Liberation of Palestine is an Individual Duty:

Article Fifteen:

The day that enemies usurp part of Muslim land, Jihad becomes the individual duty of every Muslim. In face of the Jews' usurpation of Palestine, it is compulsory that the banner of Jihad be raised. To do this requires the diffusion of Islamic consciousness among the masses, both on the regional, Arab and Islamic levels. It is necessary to instill the spirit of Jihad in the heart of the nation so that they would confront the enemies and join the ranks of the fighters.

It is necessary that scientists, educators and teachers, information and media people, as well as the educated masses, especially the youth and sheikhs of the Islamic movements, should take part in the operation of awakening (the masses). It is important that basic changes be made in the school curriculum, to cleanse it of the traces of ideological invasion that affected it as a result of the orientalists and missionaries who infiltrated the region following the defeat of the Crusaders at the hands of Salah el-Din (Saladin). The Crusaders maintained that it was impossible to defeat the Muslims without first having ideological invasion pave the way by upsetting their thoughts, disfiguring their heritage and violating their ideals. Only then could they invade with soldiers. This, in its turn, paved the way for the imperialistic invasion that made Allenby declare on entering Jerusalem: "Only now have the Crusades ended." General Guru stood at Salah el-Din's grave and said: "We have returned, O Salah el-Din." Imperialism has helped towards the strengthening of ideological invasion, deepening, and still does, its roots. All this has paved the way towards the loss of Palestine.

It is necessary to instill in the minds of the Muslim generations that the Palestinian problem is a religious problem, and should be dealt with on this basis. Palestine contains Islamic holy sites. In it there is al-Aqsa Mosque which is bound to the great Mosque in Mecca in an inseparable bond as long as heaven and earth speak of Isra (Mohammed's midnight journey to the seven heavens) and Mi'raj (Mohammed's ascension to the seven heavens from Jerusalem).

"The bond of one day for the sake of Allah is better than the world and whatever there is on it. The place of one's whip in Paradise is far better than the world and whatever there is on it. A worshipper's going and coming in the service of Allah is better than the world and whatever there is on it." (As related by al-Bukhari, Muslim, al-Tarmdhi and Ibn Maja).

"I swear by the holder of Mohammed's soul that I would like to invade and be killed for the sake of Allah, then invade and be killed, and then invade again and be killed." (As related by al-Bukhari and Muslim).

The Education of the Generations:

Article Sixteen:

It is necessary to follow Islamic orientation in educating the Islamic generations in our region by teaching the religious duties, comprehensive study of the Koran, the study of the Prophet's Sunna (his sayings and doings), and learning about Islamic history and heritage from their authentic sources. This should be done by specialized and learned people, using a curriculum that would healthily form the thoughts and faith of the Muslim student. Side by side with this, a comprehensive study of the enemy, his human and financial capabilities, learning about his points of weakness and strength, and getting to know the forces supporting and helping him, should also be included. Also, it is important to be acquainted with the current events, to follow what is new and to study the analysis and commentaries made of these events. Planning for the present and future, studying every trend appearing, is a must so that the fighting Muslim would live knowing his aim, objective and his way in the midst of what is going on around him.

"O my son, verily every matter, whether good or bad, though it be the weight of a grain of mustard-seed, and be hidden in a rock, or in the heavens, or in the earth, Allah will bring the same to light; for Allah is clear-sighted and knowing. O my son, be constant at prayer, and command that which is just, and forbid that which is evil: and be patient under the afflictions which shall befall thee; for this is a duty absolutely incumbent on all men. Distort not thy face out of contempt to men, neither walk in the earth with insolence; for Allah loveth no arrogant, vain-glorious person." (Lokman – verses 16-18).

The Role of the Muslim Woman:

Article Seventeen:

The Muslim woman has a role no less important than that of the Muslim man in the battle of liberation. She is the maker of men. Her role in guiding and educating the new generations is great. The enemies have realized the importance of her role. They consider that if they are able to direct and bring her up they way they wish, far from Islam, they would have won the battle. That is why you find them giving these attempts constant attention through information campaigns, films, and the school curriculum, using for that purpose their lackeys who are infiltrated through Zionist organizations under various names and shapes, such as Freemasons, Rotary Clubs, espionage groups and others, which are all nothing more than cells of subversion and saboteurs. These organizations have ample resources that enable them to play their role in societies for the purpose of achieving the Zionist targets and to deepen the concepts that would serve the enemy. These organizations operate in the absence of Islam and its estrangement among its people. The Islamic peoples should perform their role in confronting the conspiracies of these saboteurs. The day Islam is in control of guiding the affairs of life, these organizations, hostile to humanity and Islam, will be obliterated.

Article Eighteen:

Woman in the home of the fighting family, whether she is a mother or a sister, plays the most important role in looking after the family, rearing the children and imbuing them with moral values and thoughts derived from Islam. She has to teach them to perform the religious duties in preparation for the role of fighting awaiting them. That is why it is necessary to pay great attention to schools and the curriculum followed in educating Muslim girls, so that they would grow up to be good mothers, aware of their role in the battle of liberation.

She has to be of sufficient knowledge and understanding where the performance of housekeeping matters are concerned, because economy and avoidance of waste of the family budget, is one of the requirements for the ability to continue moving forward in the difficult conditions surrounding us. She should put before her eyes the fact that the money available to her is just like blood which should never flow except through the veins so that both children and grown-ups could continue to live.

"Verily, the Muslims of either sex, and the true believers of either sex, and the devout men, and the devout women, and the men of veracity, and the women of veracity, and the patient men, and the patient women, and the humble men, and the humble women, and the alms-givers of either sex who remember Allah frequently; for them hath Allah prepared forgiveness and a great reward." (The Confederates – verse 25).

The Role of Islamic Art in the Battle of Liberation:

Article Nineteen:

Art has regulations and measures by which it can be determined whether it is Islamic or pre-Islamic (Jahili) art. The issues of Islamic liberation are in need of Islamic art that would take the spirit high, without raising one side of human nature above the other, but rather raise all of them harmoniously an in equilibrium.

Man is a unique and wonderful creature, made out of a handful of clay and a breath from Allah. Islamic art addresses man on this basis, while pre-Islamic art addresses the body giving preference to the clay component in it.

The book, the article, the bulletin, the sermon, the thesis, the popular poem, the poetic ode, the song, the play and others, contain the characteristics of Islamic art, then these are among the requirements of ideological mobilization, renewed food for the journey and recreation for the soul. The road is long and suffering is plenty. The soul will be bored, but Islamic art renews the energies, resurrects the movement, arousing in them lofty meanings and proper conduct. "Nothing can improve the self if it is in retreat except shifting from one mood to another."

All this is utterly serious and no jest, for those who are fighters do not jest.

Social Mutual Responsibility:

Article Twenty:

Muslim society is a mutually responsible society. The Prophet, prayers and greetings be unto him, said: "Blessed are the generous, whether they were in town or on a journey, who have collected all that they had and shared it equally among themselves."

The Islamic spirit is what should prevail in every Muslim society. The society that confronts a vicious enemy which acts in a way similar to Nazism, making no differentiation between man and woman, between children and old people – such a society is entitled to this Islamic spirit. Our enemy relies on the methods of collective punishment. He has deprived people of their homeland and properties, pursued them in their places of exile and gathering, breaking bones, shooting at women, children and old people, with or without a reason. The enemy has opened detention camps where thousands and thousands of people are thrown and kept under sub-human conditions. Added to this, are the demolition of houses, rendering children orphans, meting cruel sentences against thousands of young people, and causing them to spend the best years of their lives in the dungeons of prisons.

In their Nazi treatment, the Jews made no exception for women or children. Their policy of striking fear in the heart is meant for all. They attack people where their breadwinning is concerned, extorting their money and threatening their honor. They deal with people as if they were the worst war criminals. Deportation from the homeland is a kind of murder.

To counter these deeds, it is necessary that social mutual responsibility should prevail among the people. The enemy should be faced by the people as a single body which if one member of it should complain, the rest of the body would respond by feeling the same pains.

Article Twenty-One:

Mutual social responsibility means extending assistance, financial or moral, to all those who are in need and joining in the execution of some of the work. Members of the Islamic Resistance Movement should consider the interests of the masses as their own personal interests. They must spare no effort in achieving and preserving them. They must prevent any foul play with the future of the upcoming generations and anything that could cause loss to society. The masses are part of them and they are part of the masses. Their strength is theirs, and their future is theirs. Members of the Islamic Resistance Movement should share the people's joy and grief, adopt the demands of the public and whatever means by which they could be realized. The day that such a spirit prevails, brotherliness would deepen, cooperation, sympathy and unity will be enhanced and the ranks will be solidified to confront the enemies.

Supportive Forces Behind the Enemy:

Article Twenty-Two:

For a long time, the enemies have been planning, skillfully and with precision, for the achievement of what they have attained. They took into consideration the causes affecting the current of events. They strived to amass great and substantive material wealth which they devoted to the realization of their dream. With their money, they took control of the world media, news agencies, the press, publishing houses, broadcasting stations, and others. With their money they stirred revolutions in various parts of the world with the purpose of achieving their interests and reaping the fruit therein. They were behind the French Revolution, the Communist revolution and most of the revolutions we heard and hear about, here and there. With their money they formed secret societies, such as Freemasons, 2 Clubs, the Lions and others in different parts of the world for the purpose of sabotaging societies and achieving Zionist interests. With their money they were able to control imperialistic countries and instigate them to colonize many countries in order to enable them to exploit their resources and spread corruption there.

You may speak as much as you want about regional and world wars. They were behind World War I, when they were able to destroy the Islamic Caliphate, making financial gains and controlling resources. They obtained the Balfour Declaration, formed the League of Nations through which they could rule the world. They were behind World War II, through which they made huge financial gains by trading in armaments, and paved the way for the establishment of their state. It was they who instigated the replacement of the League of Nations with the United Nations and the Security Council to enable them to rule the world through them. There is no war going on anywhere, without having their finger in it.

"So often as they shall kindle a fire for war, Allah shall extinguish it; and they shall set their minds to act corruptly in the earth, but Allah loveth not the corrupt doers." (The Table – verse 64).

The imperialistic forces in the Capitalist West and Communist East support the enemy with all their might, in money and in men. These forces take turns in doing that. The day Islam appears, the forces of infidelity would unite to challenge it, for the infidels are of one nation.

"O true believers, contract not an intimate friendship with any besides yourselves: they will not fail to corrupt you. They wish for that which may cause you to perish: their hatred hath already appeared from out of their mouths; but what their breasts conceal is yet more inveterate. We have already shown you signs of their ill will towards you, if ye understand." (The Family of Imran – verse 118).

It is not in vain that the verse is ended with Allah's words "if ye understand."

Our Attitudes Towards:

F. Islamic Movements:

Article Twenty-Three:

The Islamic Resistance Movement views other Islamic movements with respect and appreciation. If it were at variance with them on one point or opinion, it is in agreement with them on other points and understandings. It considers these movements, if they reveal good intentions and dedication to Allah, that they fall into the category of those who are trying hard since they act within the Islamic circle. Each active person has his share.

The Islamic Resistance Movement considers all these movements as a fund for itself. It prays to Allah for guidance and directions for all and it spares no effort to keep the banner of unity raised, ever striving for its realization in accordance with the Koran and the Prophet's directives.

"And cleave all of you unto the covenant of Allah, and depart not from it, and remember the favour of Allah towards you: since ye were enemies, and he reconciled your hearts, and ye became companions and brethren by his favour: and ye were on the brink of a pit of fire, and he delivered you thence. Allah declareth unto you his signs, that ye may be directed." (The Family of Imran – Verse 102).

Article Twenty-Four:

The Islamic Resistance Movement does not allow slandering or speaking ill of individuals or groups, for the believer does not indulge in such malpractices. It is necessary to differentiate between this behavior and the stands taken by certain individuals and groups. Whenever those stands are erroneous, the Islamic Resistance Movement preserves the right to expound the error and to warn against it. It will strive to show the right path and to judge the case in question with objectivity. Wise conduct is indeed the target of the believer who follows it wherever he discerns it.

"Allah loveth not the speaking ill of anyone in public, unless he who is injured call for assistance; and Allah heareth and knoweth: whether ye publish a good action, or conceal it, or forgive evil, verily Allah is gracious and powerful." (Women – verses 147-148).

B. Nationalist Movements in the Palestinian Arena:

Article Twenty-Five:

The Islamic Resistance Movement respects these movements and appreciates their circumstances and the conditions surrounding and affecting them. It encourages them as long as they do not give their allegiance to the Communist East or the Crusading West. It confirms to all those who are integrated in it, or sympathetic towards it, that the Islamic Resistance Movement is a fighting movement that has a moral and enlightened look of life and the way it should cooperate with the other (movements). It detests opportunism and desires only the good of people, individuals and groups alike. It does not seek material gains, personal fame, nor does it look for a reward from others. It works with its own resources and whatever is at its disposal "and prepare for them whatever force you can," for the fulfillment of the duty, and the earning of Allah's favor. It has no other desire than that.

The Movement assures all the nationalist trends operating in the Palestinian arena for the liberation of Palestine, that it is there for their support and assistance. It will never be more than that, both in words and deeds, now and in the future. It is there to bring together and not to divide, to preserve and not to squander, to unify and not to throw asunder. It evaluates every good word, sincere effort and good offices. It closes the door in the face of side disagreements and does not lend an ear to rumors and slanders, while at the same time fully realizing the right for self-defense.

Anything contrary or contradictory to these trends, is a lie disseminated by enemies or their lackeys for the purpose of sowing confusion, disrupting the ranks and occupy them with side issues.

"O true believers, if a wicked man come unto you with a tale, inquire strictly into the truth thereof; lest ye hurt people through ignorance, and afterwards repent of what ye have done." (The Inner Apartments – verse 6).

Article Twenty-Six:

In viewing the Palestinian nationalist movements that give allegiance neither to the East nor the West, in this positive way, the Islamic Resistance Movement does not refrain from discussing new situations on the regional or international levels where the Palestinian question is concerned. It does that in such an objective manner revealing the extent of how much it is in harmony or contradiction with the national interests in the light of the Islamic point of view.

C. The Palestinian Liberation Organization:

Article Twenty-Seven:

The Palestine Liberation Organization (PLO) is the closest to the heart of the Islamic Resistance Movement. It contains the father and the brother, the next of kin and the friend. The Muslim does not estrange himself from his father, brother, next of kin or friend. Our homeland is one, our situation is one, our fate is one and the enemy is a joint enemy to all of us.

Because of the situations surrounding the formation of the Organization, of the ideological confusion prevailing in the Arab world as a result of the ideological invasion under whose influence the Arab world has fallen since the defeat of the Crusaders and which was, and still is, intensified through orientalists, missionaries and imperialists, the Organization adopted the idea of the secular state. And that it how we view it.

Secularism completely contradicts religious ideology. Attitudes, conduct and decisions stem from ideologies.

That is why, with all our appreciation for The Palestine Liberation Organization – and what it can develop into – and without belittling its role in the Arab-Israeli conflict, we are unable to exchange the present or future Islamic Palestine with the secular idea. The Islamic nature of Palestine is part of our religion and whoever takes his religion lightly is a loser.

"Who will be adverse to the religion of Abraham, but he whose mind is infatuated? (The Cow – verse 130).

The day The Palestine Liberation Organization adopts Islam as its way of life, we will become its soldiers, and fuel for its fire that will burn the enemies.

Until such a day, and we pray to Allah that it will be soon, the Islamic Resistance Movement's stand towards the PLO is that of the son towards his father, the brother towards his brother, and the relative to relative, suffers his pain and supports him in confronting the enemies, wishing him to be wise and well-guided.

"Stand by your brother, for he who is brotherless is like the fighter who goes to battle without arms. One's cousin is the wing one flies with – could the bird fly without wings?"

D. Arab and Islamic Countries:

Article Twenty-Eight:

The Zionist invasion is a vicious invasion. It does not refrain from resorting to all methods, using all evil and contemptible ways to achieve its end. It relies greatly in its infiltration and espionage operations on the secret organizations it gave rise to, such as the Freemasons, The Rotary and Lions clubs, and other sabotage groups. All these organizations, whether secret or open, work in the interest of Zionism and according to its instructions. They aim at undermining societies, destroying values, corrupting consciences, deteriorating character and annihilating Islam. It is behind the drug trade and alcoholism in all its kinds so as to facilitate its control and expansion.

Arab countries surrounding Israel are asked to open their borders before the fighters from among the Arab and Islamic nations so that they could consolidate their efforts with those of their Muslim brethren in Palestine.

As for the other Arab and Islamic countries, they are asked to facilitate the movement of the fighters from and to it, and this is the least thing they could do.

We should not forget to remind every Muslim that when the Jews conquered the Holy City in 1967, they stood on the threshold of the Aqsa Mosque and proclaimed that "Mohammed is dead, and his descendants are all women."

Israel, Judaism and Jews challenge Islam and the Muslim people. "May the cowards never sleep."

E. Nationalist and Religious Groupings, Institutions, Intellectuals, The Arab and Islamic World:

The Islamic Resistance Movement hopes that all these groupings will side with it in all spheres, would support it, adopt its stand and solidify its activities and moves, work towards rallying support for it so that the Islamic people will be a base and a stay for it, supplying it with strategic depth an all human material and informative spheres, in time and in place. This should be done through the convening of solidarity conferences, the issuing of explanatory bulletins, favorable articles and booklets, enlightening the masses regarding the Palestinian issue, clarifying what confronts it and the conspiracies woven around it. They should mobilize the Islamic nations, ideologically, educationally and culturally, so that these peoples would be equipped to perform their role in the decisive battle of liberation, just as they did when they vanquished the Crusaders and the Tatars and saved human civilization. Indeed, that is not difficult for Allah.

"Allah hath written, Verily I will prevail, and my apostles: for Allah is strong and mighty." (The Dispute – verse 21).

Article Thirty:

Writers, intellectuals, media people, orators, educators and teachers, and all the various sectors in the Arab and Islamic world – all of them are called upon to perform their role, and to fulfill their duty, because of the ferocity of the Zionist offensive and the Zionist influence in many countries exercised through financial and media control, as well as the consequences that all this lead to in the greater part of the world.

Jihad is not confined to the carrying of arms and the confrontation of the enemy. The effective word, the good article, the useful book, support and solidarity – together with the presence of sincere purpose for the hoisting of Allah's banner higher and higher – all these are elements of the Jihad for Allah's sake.

"Whosoever mobilizes a fighter for the sake of Allah is himself a fighter. Whosoever supports the relatives of a fighter, he himself is a fighter." (related by al-Bukhari, Muslim, Abu-Dawood and al-Tarmadhi).

F. Followers of Other Religions: The Islamic Resistance Movement Is A Humanistic Movement:

Article Thirty-One:

The Islamic Resistance Movement is a humanistic movement. It takes care of human rights and is guided by Islamic tolerance when dealing with the followers of other religions. It does not antagonize anyone of them except if it is antagonized by it or stands in its way to hamper its moves and waste its efforts.

Under the wing of Islam, it is possible for the followers of the three religions – Islam, Christianity and Judaism – to coexist in peace and quiet with each other. Peace and quiet would not be possible except under the wing of Islam. Past and present history are the best witness to that.

It is the duty of the followers of other religions to stop disputing the sovereignty of Islam in this region, because the day these followers should take over there will be nothing but carnage, displacement and terror. Every one of them is at variance with his fellow-religionists, not to speak about followers of other religionists. Past and present history are full of examples to prove this fact.

"They will not fight against you in a body, except in fenced towns, or from behind walls. Their strength in war among themselves is great: thou thinkest them to be united; but their hearts are divided. This, because they are people who do not understand." (The Emigration – verse 14).

Islam confers upon everyone his legitimate rights. Islam prevents the incursion on other people's rights. The Zionist Nazi activities against our people will not last for long. "For the state of injustice lasts but one day, while the state of justice lasts till Doomsday."

"As to those who have not borne arms against you on account of religion, nor turned you out of your dwellings, Allah forbiddeth you not to deal kindly with them, and to behave justly towards them; for Allah loveth those who act justly." (The Tried – verse 8).

The Attempt to Isolate the Palestinian People:

Article Thirty-Two:

World Zionism, together with imperialistic powers, try through a studied plan and an intelligent strategy to remove one Arab state after another from the circle of struggle against Zionism, in order to have it finally face the Palestinian people only. Egypt was, to a great extent, removed from the circle of the struggle, through the treacherous Camp David Agreement. They are trying to draw other Arab countries into similar agreements and to bring them outside the circle of struggle.

The Islamic Resistance Movement calls on Arab and Islamic nations to take up the line of serious and persevering action to prevent the success of this horrendous plan, to warn the people of the danger emanating from leaving the circle of struggle against Zionism. Today it is Palestine, tomorrow it will be one country or another. The Zionist plan is limitless. After Palestine, the Zionists aspire to expand from the Nile to the Euphrates. When they will have digested the region they overtook, they will aspire to further expansion, and so on. Their plan is embodied in the "Protocols of the Elders of Zion," and their present conduct is the best proof of what we are saying.

Leaving the circle of struggle with Zionism is high treason, and cursed be he who does that. "for whoso shall turn his back unto them on that day, unless he turneth aside to fight, or retreateth to another party of the faithful, shall draw on himself the indignation of Allah, and his abode shall be hell; an ill journey shall it be thither." (The Spoils – verse 16). There is no way out except by concentrating all powers and energies to face this Nazi, vicious Tatar invasion. The alternative is loss of one's country, the dispersion of citizens, the spread of vice on earth and the destruction of religious values. Let every person know that he is responsible before Allah, for "the doer of the slightest good deed is rewarded in like, and the doer of the slightest evil deed is also rewarded in like."

The Islamic Resistance Movement considers itself to be the spearhead of the circle of struggle with world Zionism and a step on the road. The Movement adds its efforts to the efforts of all those who are active in the Palestinian arena. Arab and Islamic Peoples should augment by further steps on their part; Islamic groupings all over the Arab world should also do the same, since all of these are the best equipped for the future role in the fight with the warmongering Jews.

"... and we have put enmity and hatred between them, until the day of resurrection. So often as they shall kindle a fire of war, Allah shall extinguish it; and they shall set their minds to act corruptly in the earth, but Allah loveth not the corrupt doers." (The Table – verse 64).

Article Thirty-Three:

The Islamic Resistance Movement, being based on the common coordinated and interdependent conceptions of the laws of the universe, and flowing in the stream of destiny in confronting and fighting the enemies in defence of the Muslims and Islamic civilization and sacred sites, the first among which is the Aqsa Mosque, urges the Arab and Islamic peoples, their governments, popular and official groupings, to fear Allah where their view of the Islamic Resistance Movement and their dealings with it are concerned. They should back and support it, as Allah wants them to, extending to it more and more funds till Allah's purpose is achieved when ranks will close up, fighters join other fighters and masses everywhere in the Islamic world will come forward in response to the call of duty while loudly proclaiming: Hail to Jihad. Their cry will reach the heavens and will go on being resounded until liberation is achieved, the invaders vanquished and Allah's victory comes about.

"And Allah will certainly assist him who shall be on his side: for Allah is strong and mighty." (The Pilgrimage – verse 40).

The Testimony of History

Across History in Confronting the Invaders:

Article Thirty-Four:

Palestine is the navel of the globe and the crossroad of the continents. Since the dawn of history, it has been the target of expansionists. The Prophet, Allah bless him and grant him salvation, had himself pointed to this fact in the noble Hadith in which he called on his honorable companion, Ma'adh ben-Jabal, saying: O Ma'ath, Allah throw open before you, when I am gone, Syria, from Al-Arish to the Euphrates. Its men, women and slaves will stay firmly there till the Day of Judgment. Whoever of you should choose one of the Syrian shores, or the Holy Land, he will be in constant struggle till the Day of Judgment."

Expansionists have more than once put their eye on Palestine which they attacked with their armies to fulfill their designs on it. Thus it was that the Crusaders came with their armies, bringing with them their creed and carrying their Cross. They were able to defeat the Muslims for a while, but the Muslims were able to retrieve the land only when they stood under the wing of their religious banner, united their word, hallowed the name of Allah and surged out fighting under the leadership of Salah ed-Din al-Ayyubi. They fought for almost twenty years and at the end the Crusaders were defeated and Palestine was liberated.

"Say unto those who believe not, Ye shall be overcome, and thrown together into hell; an unhappy couch it shall be." (The Family of Imran – verse 12).

This is the only way to liberate Palestine. There is no doubt about the testimony of history. It is one of the laws of the universe and one of the rules of existence. Nothing can overcome iron except iron. Their false futile creed can only be defeated by the righteous Islamic creed. A creed could not be fought except by a creed, and in the last analysis, victory is for the just, for justice is certainly victorious.

"Our word hath formerly been given unto our servants the apostles; that they should certainly be assisted against the infidels, and that our armies should surely be the conquerors." (Those Who Rank Themselves – verses 171-172).

Article Thirty-Five:

The Islamic Resistance Movement views seriously the defeat of the Crusaders at the hands of Salah ed-Din al-Ayyubi and the rescuing of Palestine from their hands, as well as the defeat of the Tatars at Ein Galot, breaking their power at the hands of Qataz and Al-Dhaher Bivers and saving the Arab world from the Tatar onslaught which aimed at the destruction of every meaning of human civilization. The Movement draws lessons and examples from all this. The present Zionist onslaught has also been preceded by Crusading raids from the West and other Tatar raids from the East. Just as the Muslims faced those raids and planned fighting and defeating them, they should be able to confront the Zionist invasion and defeat it. This is indeed no problem for the Almighty Allah, provided that the intentions are pure, the determination is true and that

Muslims have benefited from past experiences, rid themselves of the effects of ideological invasion and followed the customs of their ancestors.

The Islamic Resistance Movement is Composed of Soldiers:

Article Thirty-Six:

While paving its way, the Islamic Resistance Movement, emphasizes time and again to all the sons of our people, to the Arab and Islamic nations, that it does not seek personal fame, material gain, or social prominence. It does not aim to compete against any one from among our people, or take his place. Nothing of the sort at all. It will not act against any of the sons of Muslims or those who are peaceful towards it from among non-Muslims, be they here or anywhere else. It will only serve as a support for all groupings and organizations operating against the Zionist enemy and its lackeys.

The Islamic Resistance Movement adopts Islam as its way of life. Islam is its creed and religion. Whoever takes Islam as his way of life, be it an organization, a grouping, a country or any other body, the Islamic Resistance Movement considers itself as their soldiers and nothing more.

We ask Allah to show us the right course, to make us an example to others and to judge between us and our people with truth. "O Lord, do thou judge between us and our nation with truth; for thou art the best judge." (Al Araf – Verse 89).

The last of our prayers will be praise to Allah, the Master of the Universe.

http://avalon.law.yale.edu/20[th]_century/Hamas.asp

APPENDIX II

A Document of General Principles and Policies

In the Name of Allah Most Gracious Most Merciful

The Islamic Resistance Movement "Hamas"

A Document of General Principles and Policies

Praise be to Allah, the Lord of all worlds. May the peace and blessings of Allah be upon Muhammad, the Master of Messengers and the Leader of the mujahidin, and upon his household and all his companions.

Preamble:

Palestine is the land of the Arab Palestinian people, from it they originate, to it they adhere and belong, and about it they reach out and communicate.

Palestine is a land whose status has been elevated by Islam, a faith that holds it in high esteem, that breathes through it its spirit and just values and that lays the foundation for the doctrine of defending and protecting it.

Palestine is the cause of a people who have been let down by a world that fails to secure their rights and restore to them what has been usurped from them, a people whose land continues to suffer one of the worst types of occupation in this world.

Palestine is a land that was seized by a racist, anti-human and colonial Zionist project that was founded on a false promise (the Balfour Declaration), on recognition of a usurping entity and on imposing a fait accompli by force.

Palestine symbolizes the resistance that shall continue until liberation is accomplished, until the return is fulfilled and until a fully sovereign state is established with Jerusalem as its capital.

Palestine is the true partnership among Palestinians of all affiliations for the sublime objective of liberation.

Palestine is the spirit of the Ummah and its central cause; it is the soul of humanity and its living conscience.

This document is the product of deep deliberations that led us to a strong consensus. As a movement, we agree about both the theory and the practice of the vision that is outlined in the pages that follow. It is a vision that stands on solid grounds and on well-established principles. This document unveils the goals, the milestones and the way in which national unity can be enforced. It also establishes our common understanding of the Palestinian cause, the working principles which we use to further it, and the limits of flexibility used to interpret it.

The Movement:

1. The Islamic Resistance Movement "Hamas" is a Palestinian Islamic national liberation and resistance movement. Its goal is to liberate Palestine and confront the Zionist project. Its frame of reference is Islam, which determines its principles, objectives and means.

The Land of Palestine:

2. Palestine, which extends from the River Jordan in the east to the Mediterranean in the west and from Ras Al-Naqurah in the north to Umm Al-Rashrash in the south, is an integral territorial unit. It is the land and the home of the Palestinian people. The expulsion and banishment of the Palestinian people from their land and the establishment of the Zionist entity therein do not annul the right of the Palestinian people to their entire land and do not entrench any rights therein for the usurping Zionist entity.

3. Palestine is an Arab Islamic land. It is a blessed sacred land that has a special place in the heart of every Arab and every Muslim.

The Palestinian People:

4. The Palestinians are the Arabs who lived in Palestine until 1947, irrespective of whether they were expelled from it, or stayed in it; and every person that was born to an Arab Palestinian father after that date, whether inside or outside Palestine, is a Palestinian.

5. The Palestinian identity is authentic and timeless; it is passed from generation to generation. The catastrophes that have befallen the Palestinian people, as a consequence of the Zionist occupation and its policy of displacement, cannot erase the identity of the Palestinian people nor can they negate it. A Palestinian shall not lose his or her national identity or rights by acquiring a second nationality.

6. The Palestinian people are one people, made up of all Palestinians, inside and outside of Palestine, irrespective of their religion, culture or political affiliation.

Islam and Palestine:

7. Palestine is at the heart of the Arab and Islamic Ummah and enjoys a special status. Within Palestine there exists Jerusalem, whose precincts are blessed by Allah. Palestine is the Holy Land, which Allah has blessed for humanity. It is the Muslims' first Qiblah and the destination of the journey performed at night by Prophet Muhammad, peace be upon him. It is the location from where he ascended to the upper heavens. It is the birthplace of Jesus Christ, peace be upon him. Its soil contains the remains of thousands of Prophets, Companions and Mujahidin. It is the land of people who are determined to defend the truth – within Jerusalem and its surroundings – who are not deterred

or intimidated by those who oppose them and by those who betray them, and they will continue their mission until the Promise of Allah is fulfilled.

8. By virtue of its justly balanced middle way and moderate spirit, Islam – for Hamas - provides a comprehensive way of life and an order that is fit for purpose at all times and in all places. Islam is a religion of peace and tolerance. It provides an umbrella for the followers of other creeds and religions who can practice their beliefs in security and safety. Hamas also believes that Palestine has always been and will always be a model of coexistence, tolerance and civilizational innovation.

9. Hamas believes that the message of Islam upholds the values of truth, justice, freedom and dignity and prohibits all forms of injustice and incriminates oppressors irrespective of their religion, race, gender or nationality. Islam is against all forms of religious, ethnic or sectarian extremism and bigotry. It is the religion that inculcates in its followers the value of standing up to aggression and of supporting the oppressed; it motivates them to give generously and make sacrifices in defence of their dignity, their land, their peoples and their holy places.

Jerusalem:

10. Jerusalem is the capital of Palestine. Its religious, historic and civilizational status is fundamental to the Arabs, Muslims and the world at large. Its Islamic and Christian holy places belong exclusively to the Palestinian people and to the Arab and Islamic Ummah. Not one stone of Jerusalem can be surrendered or relinquished. The measures undertaken by the occupiers in Jerusalem, such as Judaization, settlement building, and establishing facts on the ground are fundamentally null and void.

11. The blessed Al-Aqsa Mosque belongs exclusively to our people and our Ummah, and the occupation has no right to it whatsoever. The occupation's plots, measures and attempts to judaize Al-Aqsa and divide it are null, void and illegitimate.

The Refugees and the Right of Return:

12. The Palestinian cause in its essence is a cause of an occupied land and a displaced people. The right of the Palestinian refugees and the displaced to return to their homes from which they were banished or were banned from returning to – whether in the lands occupied in 1948 or in 1967 (that is the whole of Palestine), is a natural right, both individual and collective. This right is confirmed by all divine laws as well as by the basic principles of human rights and international law. It is an inalienable right and cannot be dispensed with by any party, whether Palestinian, Arab or international.

13. Hamas rejects all attempts to erase the rights of the refugees, including the attempts to settle them outside Palestine and through the projects of the alternative homeland. Compensation to the Palestinian refugees for the harm they have suffered as a consequence of banishing them and occupying their land is an absolute right that goes hand in hand with their right to return. They are to

receive compensation upon their return and this does not negate or diminish their right to return.

The Zionist Project:

14. The Zionist project is a racist, aggressive, colonial and expansionist project based on seizing the properties of others; it is hostile to the Palestinian people and to their aspiration for freedom, liberation, return and self-determination. The Israeli entity is the plaything of the Zionist project and its base of aggression.

15. The Zionist project does not target the Palestinian people alone; it is the enemy of the Arab and Islamic Ummah posing a grave threat to its security and interests. It is also hostile to the Ummah's aspirations for unity, renaissance and liberation and has been the major source of its troubles. The Zionist project also poses a danger to international security and peace and to mankind and its interests and stability.

16. Hamas affirms that its conflict is with the Zionist project not with the Jews because of their religion. Hamas does not wage a struggle against the Jews because they are Jewish but wages a struggle against the Zionists who occupy Palestine. Yet, it is the Zionists who constantly identify Judaism and the Jews with their own colonial project and illegal entity.

17. Hamas rejects the persecution of any human being or the undermining of his or her rights on nationalist, religious or sectarian grounds. Hamas is of the view that the Jewish problem, anti-Semitism and the persecution of the Jews are phenomena fundamentally linked to European history and not to the history of the Arabs and the Muslims or to their heritage. The Zionist movement, which was able with the help of Western powers to occupy Palestine, is the most dangerous form of settlement occupation which has already disappeared from much of the world and must disappear from Palestine.

The position toward Occupation and Political Solutions:

18. The following are considered null and void: the Balfour Declaration, the British Mandate Document, the UN Palestine Partition Resolution, and whatever resolutions and measures that derive from them or are similar to them. The establishment of "Israel" is entirely illegal and contravenes the inalienable rights of the Palestinian people and goes against their will and the will of the Ummah; it is also in violation of human rights that are guaranteed by international conventions, foremost among them is the right to self-determination.

19. There shall be no recognition of the legitimacy of the Zionist entity. Whatever has befallen the land of Palestine in terms of occupation, settlement building, Judaization or changes to its features or falsification of facts is illegitimate. Rights never lapse.

20. Hamas believes that no part of the land of Palestine shall be compromised or conceded, irrespective of the causes, the circumstances and the

pressures and no matter how long the occupation lasts. Hamas rejects any alternative to the full and complete liberation of Palestine, from the river to the sea. However, without compromising its rejection of the Zionist entity and without relinquishing any Palestinian rights, Hamas considers the establishment of a fully sovereign and independent Palestinian state, with Jerusalem as its capital along the lines of the 4th of June 1967, with the return of the refugees and the displaced to their homes from which they were expelled, to be a formula of national consensus.

21. Hamas affirms that the Oslo Accords and their addenda contravene the governing rules of international law in that they generate commitments that violate the inalienable rights of the Palestinian people. Therefore, the Movement rejects these agreements and all that flows from them, such as the obligations that are detrimental to the interests of our people, especially security coordination (collaboration).

22. Hamas rejects all the agreements, initiatives and settlement projects that are aimed at undermining the Palestinian cause and the rights of our Palestinian people. In this regard, any stance, initiative or political programme must not in any way violate these rights and should not contravene them or contradict them.

23. Hamas stresses that transgression against the Palestinian people, usurping their land and banishing them from their homeland cannot be called peace. Any settlements reached on this basis will not lead to peace. Resistance and jihad for the liberation of Palestine will remain a legitimate right, a duty and an honour for all the sons and daughters of our people and our Ummah.

Resistance and Liberation:

24. The liberation of Palestine is the duty of the Palestinian people in particular and the duty of the Arab and Islamic Ummah in general. It is also a humanitarian obligation as necessitated by the dictates of truth and justice. The agencies working for Palestine, whether national, Arab, Islamic or humanitarian, complement each other and are harmonious and not in conflict with each other.

25. Resisting the occupation with all means and methods is a legitimate right guaranteed by divine laws and by international norms and laws. At the heart of these lies armed resistance, which is regarded as the strategic choice for protecting the principles and the rights of the Palestinian people.

26. Hamas rejects any attempt to undermine the resistance and its arms. It also affirms the right of our people to develop the means and mechanisms of resistance. Managing resistance, in terms of escalation or de-escalation, or in terms of diversifying the means and methods, is an integral part of the process of managing the conflict and should not be at the expense of the principle of resistance.

The Palestinian Political System:

27. A real state of Palestine is a state that has been liberated. There is no alternative to a fully sovereign Palestinian State on the entire national Palestinian soil, with Jerusalem as its capital.

28. Hamas believes in, and adheres to, managing its Palestinian relations on the basis of pluralism, democracy, national partnership, acceptance of the other and the adoption of dialogue. The aim is to bolster the unity of ranks and joint action for the purpose of accomplishing national goals and fulfilling the aspirations of the Palestinian people.

29. The PLO is a national framework for the Palestinian people inside and outside of Palestine. It should therefore be preserved, developed and rebuilt on democratic foundations so as to secure the participation of all the constituents and forces of the Palestinian people, in a manner that safeguards Palestinian rights.

30. Hamas stresses the necessity of building Palestinian national institutions on sound democratic principles, foremost among them are free and fair elections. Such process should be on the basis of national partnership and in accordance with a clear programme and a clear strategy that adhere to the rights, including the right of resistance, and which fulfil the aspirations of the Palestinian people.

31. Hamas affirms that the role of the Palestinian Authority should be to serve the Palestinian people and safeguard their security, their rights and their national project.

32. Hamas stresses the necessity of maintaining the independence of Palestinian national decision-making. Outside forces should not be allowed to intervene. At the same time, Hamas affirms the responsibility of the Arabs and the Muslims and their duty and role in the liberation of Palestine from Zionist occupation.

33. Palestinian society is enriched by its prominent personalities, figures, dignitaries, civil society institutions, and youth, students, trade unionist and women's groups who together work for the achievement of national goals and societal building, pursue resistance, and achieve liberation.

34. The role of Palestinian women is fundamental in the process of building the present and the future, just as it has always been in the process of making Palestinian history. It is a pivotal role in the project of resistance, liberation and building the political system.

The Arab and Islamic Ummah:

35. Hamas believes that the Palestinian issue is the central cause for the Arab and Islamic Ummah.

36. Hamas believes in the unity of the Ummah with all its diverse constituents and is aware of the need to avoid anything that could fragment the Ummah and undermine its unity.

37. Hamas believes in cooperating with all states that support the rights of the Palestinian people. It opposes intervention in the internal affairs of any country. It also refuses to be drawn into disputes and conflicts that take place among different countries. Hamas adopts the policy of opening up to different states in the world, especially the Arab and Islamic states. It endeavours to establish balanced relations on the basis of combining the requirements of the Palestinian cause and the Palestinian people's interests on the one hand with the interests of the Ummah, its renaissance and its security on the other.

The Humanitarian and International Aspect:

38. The Palestinian issue is one that has major humanitarian and international dimensions. Supporting and backing this cause is a humanitarian and civilizational task that is required by the prerequisites of truth, justice and common humanitarian values.

39. From a legal and humanitarian perspective, the liberation of Palestine is a legitimate activity, it is an act of self-defence, and it is the expression of the natural right of all peoples to self-determination.

40. In its relations with world nations and peoples, Hamas believes in the values of cooperation, justice, freedom and respect of the will of the people.

41. Hamas welcomes the stances of states, organisations and institutions that support the rights of the Palestinian people. It salutes the free peoples of the world who support the Palestinian cause. At the same time, it denounces the support granted by any party to the Zionist entity or the attempts to cover up its crimes and aggression against the Palestinians and calls for the prosecution of Zionist war criminals.

42. Hamas rejects the attempts to impose hegemony on the Arab and Islamic Ummah just as it rejects the attempts to impose hegemony on the rest of the world's nations and peoples. Hamas also condemns all forms of colonialism, occupation, discrimination, oppression and aggression in the world.

May 2017

http://hamas.ps/ar/uploads/documents/06c77206ce934064ab5a901fa8bfef44.pdf

APPENDIX III

In the name of God, the Beneficent, the Merciful

Thanks be to God, Lord of the Two Worlds

Prayers and peace be upon the master of the Messengers

An Explanatory Memorandum

On The General Strategic Goal For The Group In North America

5/22/1991

In the name of God, the Beneficent, the Merciful
Thanks be to God, Lord of the Two Worlds
And Blessed are the Pious

5/22/1991

The beloved brother/The General Masul, may God keep him
The beloved brother/secretary of the Shura Council, may God keep him
The beloved brothers/Members of the Shura Council, may God keep them
God's peace, mercy and blessings be upon you . . . . To proceed,

I ask Almighty God that you, your families and those whom you love around you are in the best of conditions, pleasing to God, glorified His name be.

I send this letter of mine to you hoping that it would seize your attention and receive your good care as you are the people of responsibility and those to whom trust is given. Between your hands is an "Explanatory Memorandum" which I put effort in writing down so that it is not locked in the chest and the mind, and so that I can share with you a portion of the responsibility in leading the Group in this country .

What might have encouraged me to submit the memorandum in this time in particular is my feeling of a *"glimpse of hope"* and the beginning of good tidings which bring the good news that we have embarked on a new stage of Islamic activism stages in this continent.

The papers which are between your hands are not abundant extravagance, imaginations or hallucinations which passed in the mind of one of your brothers, but they are rather hopes, ambitions and challenges that I hope that you share some or most of which with me. I do not claim their infallibility or absolute correctness, but they are an at- tempt which requires study, outlook, detailing and rooting from you.

My request to my brothers is to read the memorandum and to write what they wanted of comments and corrections, keeping in mind that what is between your hands is not strange or a new submission without a root, but rather an attempt to interpret and explain some of what came in the long-term plan which we approved and adopted in our council and our conference in the year (1987).

So, my honorable brother, do not rush to throw these papers away due to your many occupations and worries, All what I'm asking of you is to read them and to comment on them hoping that we might continue together the project of our plan and our Islamic work in this part of the world. Should you do that, I would be thankful and grateful to you.

I also ask my honorable brother, the Secretary of the Council, to add the subject of the memorandum on the Council agenda in its coming meeting.

May God reward you good and keep you for His Daw'a

Your brother Mohamed Akram

In the name of God, the Beneficent, the Merciful

Thanks be to God, Lord of the Two Worlds

And Blessed are the Pious

Subject: A project for an explanatory memorandum for the General Strategic goal for the Group in North America mentioned in the long- term plan

One: The Memorandum is derived from:

The general strategic goal of the Group in America which was approved by the Shura Council and the Organizational Conference for the year [1987] is "Enablement of Islam in North America, meaning: establishing an effective and a stable Islamic Movement led by the Muslim Brotherhood which adopts Muslims' causes domestically and globally, and which works to expand the observant Muslim base, aims at unifying and directing Muslims' efforts, presents Islam as a civilization alternative, and supports the global Islamic State wherever it is ".

2 - The priority that is approved by the Shura Council for the work of the Group in its current and former session which is "Settlement".

3 - The positive development with the brothers in the Islamic Circle in an attempt to reach a unity of merger.

4 -The constant need for thinking and future planning, an attempt to read it and working to "shape" the present to comply and suit the needs and challenges of the future.

5 - The paper of his eminence, the General Masul, may God keep him, which he recently sent to the members of the Council.

Two: An Introduction to the Explanatory Memorandum:

In order to begin with the explanation, we must "summon" the following question and place it in front of our eyes as its relationship is important and necessary with the strategic goal and the explanation project we are embarking on. The question we are facing is: "How do you like to see the Islam Movement in North America in ten years?", or "taking along" the following sentence when planning and working, "Islamic Work in North America in the year (2000): A Strategic Vision".

Also, we must summon and take along "elements" of the general strategic goal of the Group in North America and I will intention- ally repeat them in numbers. They are:

[1 - Establishing an effective and stable Islamic Movement led by the Muslim Brotherhood.
2 - Adopting Muslims' causes domestically and globally.
3 - Expanding the observant Muslim base.

4- Unifying and directing Muslims' efforts.

5 - Presenting Islam as a civilization alternative

6 - Supporting the establishment of the global Islamic State wherever it is].

- It must be stressed that it has become clear and emphatically known that all is in agreement that we must *"settle"* or *"enable"* Islam and its Movement in this part of the world.

- Therefore, a joint understanding of the meaning of settlement or enablement must be adopted, through which and on whose basis we explain the general strategic goal with its six elements for the Group in North America.

<u>Three: The Concept of Settlement:</u>

This term was mentioned in the Group's *"dictionary"* and documents with various meanings in spite of the fact that everyone meant one thing with it. We believe that the understanding of the essence is the same and we will attempt here to give the word and its *"meanings"* a practical explanation with a practical Movement tone, and not a philosophical linguistic explanation, while stressing that this explanation of ours is not complete until our explanation of *"the process"* of settlement itself is understood which is mentioned in the following paragraph. We briefly say the following:

Settlement: "That Islam and its Movement become a part of the homeland it lives in".

Establishment: "That Islam turns into firmly-rooted organizations on whose bases civilization, structure and testimony are built".

Stability: "That Islam is stable in the land on which its people move".

Enablement: "That Islam is enabled within the souls, minds and the lives of the people of the country in which it moves".

Rooting: "That Islam is resident and not a passing thing, or rooted "entrenched" in the soil of the spot where it moves and not a strange plant to it".

<u>Four: The Process of Settlement:</u>

- In order for Islam and its Movement to become *"a part of the homeland"* in which it lives, *"stable"* in its land, *"rooted"* in the spirits and minds of its people, *"enabled"* in the live of its society and has firmly-established *"organizations"* on which the Islamic structure is built and with which the testimony of civilization is achieved, the Movement must plan and struggle to obtain *"the keys"* and the tools of this process in carry out this grand mission as a *"Civilization Jihadist"* responsibility which lies on the shoulders of Muslims and - on top of them - the Muslim Brotherhood in this country . Among these keys and tools are the following:

1- Adopting the concept of settlement and understanding its practical meanings:

The Explanatory Memorandum focused on the Movement and the realistic dimension of the process of settlement and its practical meanings without paying attention to the difference in understanding between the resident and the non-resident, or who is the settled and the non-settled and we believe that what was mentioned in the long-term plan in that regards suffices.

2 - Making a fundamental shift in our thinking and mentality in order to suit the challenges of the settlement mission.

What is meant with the shift - which is a positive expression - is responding to the grand challenges of the settlement issues. We believe that any transforming response begins with the method of thinking and its center, the brain, first. In order to clarify what is meant

with the shift as a key to qualify us to enter the field of settlement, we say very briefly that the following must be accomplished:

- A shift from the "amputated" partial thinking mentality to the "continuous" comprehensive mentality.
- A shift from the mentality of caution and reservation to the mentality of risk and controlled liberation.
- A shift from the mentality of the elite Movement to the mentality of the popular Movement.
- A shift from the mentality of preaching and guidance to the mentality of building and testimony
- A shift from the single opinion mentality to the multiple opinion mentality.
- A shift from the collision mentality to the absorption mentality.
- A shift from the individual mentality to the team mentality.
- A shift from the anticipation mentality to the initiative mentality.
- A shift from the hesitation mentality to the decisiveness mentality.
- A shift from the principles mentality to the programs mentality.
- A shift from the abstract ideas mentality the true organizations mentality [This is the core point and the essence of the memorandum].

3- Understanding the historical stages in which the Islamic Ikhwani activism went through in this country:

The writer of the memorandum believes that understanding and comprehending the historical stages of the Islamic activism which was led and being led by the Muslim Brotherhood in this continent is a very important key in working towards settlement, through which the Group observes its march, the direction of its movement and the curves and turns of its road. We will suffice here with mentioning the title for each of these stages [The title expresses the prevalent characteristic of the stage] [Details maybe mentioned in another future study]. Most likely , the stages are:

A - The stage of searching for self and determining the identity.
B - The stage of inner build-up and tightening the organization.

C - The stage of mosques and the Islamic centers.
D - The stage of building the Islamic organizations - the first phase.
E - The stage of building the Islamic schools - the first phase.
F - The stage of thinking about the overt Islamic Movement - the first phase.
G- The stage of openness to the other Islamic movements and attempting to reach a formula for dealing with them - the first phase.
H - The stage of reviving and establishing the Islamic organizations - the second phase. We believe that the Group is embarking on this stage in its second phase as it has to open the door and enter as it did the first time.

4- Understanding the role of the Muslim Brother in North America:

The process of settlement is a *"Civilization-Jihadist Process"* with all the word means. The Ikhwan must understand that their work in America is a kind of grand Jihad in eliminating and destroying the Western civilization from within and *"sabotaging"* its miserable house by their hands and the hands of the believers so that it is eliminated and God's religion is made victorious over all other religions. Without this level of understanding, we are not up to this challenge and have not prepared ourselves for Jihad yet. It is a Muslim's destiny to per- form Jihad and work wherever he is and wherever he lands until the final hour comes, and there is no escape from that destiny except for those who chose to slack. But, would the slackers and the Mujahedeen be equal.

5- Understanding that we cannot perform the settlement mission by ourselves or away from people:

A mission as significant and as huge as the settlement mission needs magnificent and exhausting efforts. With their capabilities, human, financial and scientific resources, the Ikhwan will not be able to carry out this mission alone or away from people and he who believes that is wrong, and God knows best. As for the role of the Ikhwan, it is the initiative, pioneering, leadership, raising the banner and pushing people in that direction. They are then to work to employ, direct and unify Muslims' efforts and powers for this process. In order to do that, we must possess a mastery of the art of *"coalitions"*, the art of *"absorption"* and the principles of *"cooperation"*.

6- The necessity of achieving a union and balanced gradual merger between private work and public work:

We believe that what was written about this subject is many and is enough. But, it needs a time and a practical frame so that what is needed is achieved in a gradual and a balanced way that is compatible with the process of settlement.

7- The conviction that the success of the settlement of Islam and its Movement in this country is a success to the global Islamic Movement and a true support for the sought- after state, God willing:

There is a conviction - with which this memorandum disagrees - that our focus in attempting to settle Islam in this country will lead to negligence in our duty towards the global Islamic Movement in supporting its project to establish the state. We believe that the reply is in two segments: One - The success of the Movement in America in establishing an observant Islamic base with power and effectiveness will be the best support and aid to the global Movement project.

And the second - is the global Movement has not succeeded yet in "distributing roles" to its branches, stating what is the needed from them as one of the participants or contributors to the project to establish the global Islamic state. The day this happens, the children of the American Ikhwani branch will have far-reaching impact and positions that make the ancestors proud.

8- Absorbing Muslims and winning them with all of their factions and colors in America and Canada for the settlement project, and making it their cause, future and the basis of their Islamic life in this part of the world:

This issue requires from us to learn "the art of dealing with the others", as people are different and people in many colors. We need to adopt the principle which says, "Take from people ... the best they have", their best specializations, experiences, arts, energies and abilities. By people here we mean those within or without the ranks of individuals and organizations. The policy of "taking" should be with what achieves the strategic goal and the settlement process. But the big challenge in front of us is: how to connect them all in "the orbit" of our plan and "the circle" of our Movement in order to achieve "the core" of our interest. To me, there is no choice for us other than alliance and mutual understanding of those who desire from our religion and those who agree from our belief in work. And the U.S. Islamic arena is full of those waiting..., the pioneers.

What matters is bringing people to the level of comprehension of the challenge that is facing us as Muslims in this country, conviction of our settlement project, and understanding the benefit of agreement, cooperation and alliance. At that time, if we ask for money, a lot of it would come, and if we ask for men, they would come in lines, What matters is that our plan is "the criterion and the balance" in our relationship with others.

Here, two points must be noted; the first one: we need to comprehend and understand the balance of the Islamic powers in the U.S. arena [and this might be the subject of a future study]. The second point: what we reached with the brothers in "ICNA" is considered a step in the right direction, the beginning of good and the first drop that requires growing and guidance.

9- Re-examining our organizational and administrative bodies, the type of leadership and the method of selecting it with what suits the challenges of the settlement mission:

The memorandum will be silent about details regarding this item even though it is logical and there is a lot to be said about it.

10- Growing and developing our resources and capabilities, our financial and human resources with what suits the magnitude of the grand mission:

If we examined the human and the financial resources the Ikhwan alone own in this country, we and others would feel proud and glorious. And if we add to them the resources of our friends and allies, those who circle in our orbit and those waiting on our banner, we would realize that we are able to open the door to settlement and walk through it seeking to make Almighty God's word the highest.

11- Utilizing the scientific method in planning, thinking and preparation of studies needed for the process of settlement:

Yes, we need this method, and we need many studies which aid in this civilization Jihadist operation. We will mention some of them briefly:

- The history of the Islamic presence in America.
- The history of the Islamic Ikhwani presence in America.
- Islamic movements, organizations and organizations: analysis and criticism.
- The phenomenon of the Islamic centers and schools: challenges, needs and statistics.
- Islamic minorities.
- Muslim and Arab communities.
- The U .S. society: make-up and politics.
- The U.S. society's view of Islam and Muslims ... And many other studies which we can direct our brothers and allies to prepare, either through their academic studies or through their educational centers or organizational task- ing. What is important is that we start.

12- Agreeing on a flexible, balanced and a clear "mechanism" to implement the process of settlement within a specific, gradual and balanced "time frame" that is in-line with the demands and challenges of the process of settlement.

13- Understanding the U.S. society from its different aspects an understanding that "qualifies" us to perform the mission of settling our Dawa' in its country "and growing it" on its land.

14- Adopting a written "jurisprudence" that includes legal and movement bases, principles, policies and interpretations which are suitable for the needs and challenges of the process of settlement.

15- Agreeing on "criteria" and balances to be a sort of "antennas" or "the watch tower" in order to make sure that all of our priorities, plans, programs, bodies, leadership, monies and activities march towards the process of the settlement.

16- Adopting a practical, flexible formula through which our central work complements our domestic work.

[Items 12 through 16 will be detailed later].

17- Understanding the role and the nature of work of *"The Islamic Center"* in every city with what achieves the goal of the process of settlement:

The center we seek is the one which constitutes the *"nexus"* of our Movement, the *"perimeter"* of the circle of our work, our *"balance center"*, the *"base"* for our rise and our *"Dar al-Arqam"* to educate us, prepare us and supply our battalions in addition to being the *"niche"* of our prayers.

This is in order for the Islamic center to turn - in action not in words - into a seed *"for a small Islamic society"* which is a reflection and a mirror to our central organizations. The center ought to turn into a *"beehive"* which produces sweet honey. Thus, the Islamic center would turn into a place for study, family, battalion, course, seminar, visit, sport, school, social club, women gathering, kindergarten for male and female youngsters, the office of the domestic political resolution, and the center for distributing our newspapers, magazines, books and our audio and visual tapes.

In brief we say: we would like for the Islamic center to be- come *"The House of Dawa'"* and *"the general center"* in deeds first before name. As much as we own and direct these centers at the continent level, we can say we are marching successfully towards the settlement of Dawa' in this country .

Meaning that the *"center's"* role should be the same as the *"mosque's"* role during the time of God's prophet, God's prayers and peace be upon him, when he marched to *"settle"* the Dawa' in its first generation in Madina. From the mosque, he drew the Islamic life and provided to the world the most magnificent and fabulous civilization humanity knew.

This mandates that, eventually, the region, the branch and the Usra turn into *"operations rooms"* for planning, direction, monitoring and leadership for the Islamic center in order to be a role model to be followed.

18- Adopting a system that is based on *"selecting"* workers, *"role distribution"* and *"assigning"* positions and responsibilities is based on specialization, desire and need with what achieves the process of settlement and contributes to its success.

19- Turning the principle of dedication for the Masuls of main positions within the Group into a rule, a basis and a policy in work. Without it, the process of settlement might be stalled [Talking about this point requires more details and discussion].

20- Understanding the importance of the *"Organizational"* shift in our Movement work, and doing Jihad in order to achieve it in the real world with what serves the process of settlement and expedites its results, God Almighty's willing:

The reason this paragraph was delayed is to stress its utmost importance as it constitutes the heart and the core of this memorandum. It also constitutes the practical aspect and the true measure of our success or failure in our march towards settlement. The talk about the organizations and the *"organizational"* mentality or phenomenon does not require much details. It suffices to say that the first pioneer of this phenomenon was our prophet Mohamed, God's peace, mercy and blessings be upon him, as he placed the foundation for the first civilized organization which is the mosque, which truly became *"the comprehensive organization"*. And this was done by the pioneer of the contemporary Islamic Dawa', Imam martyr Hasan al-Banna, may God have mercy on him, when he and his brothers felt the need to *"re-establish"* Islam and its movement anew, leading him to establish organizations with all their kinds: economic, social, media, scouting, professional and even the military ones. We must say that we are in a country which understands no language other than the language of the organizations, and one which does not respect or give weight to any group without effective, functional and strong organizations.

It is good fortune that there are brothers among us who have this *"trend"*, mentality or inclination to build the organizations who have beat us by action and words which leads us to dare say honestly what Sadat in Egypt once said, *"We want to build a country of organizations"* - a word of right he meant wrong with. I say to my brothers, let us raise the banner of truth to establish right *"We want to establish the Group of organizations"*, as without it we will not able to put our feet on the true path.

- And in order for the process of settlement to be completed, we must plan and work from now to equip and prepare ourselves, our brothers, our apparatuses, our sections and our committees in order to turn into comprehensive organizations in a gradual and balanced way that is suitable with the need and the reality. What encourages us to do that - in addition to the aforementioned - is that we possess *"seeds"* for each organization from the organization we call for [See attachment number (1)].

- All we need is to tweak them, coordinate their work, collect their elements and merge their efforts with others and then connect them with the comprehensive plan we seek. For instance, W e have a seed for a *"comprehensive media and art"* organization: we own a print + advanced typesetting machine + audio and visual center + art production office + magazines in Arabic and English [The Horizons, The Hope, The Politicians, Ila Falastine, Press Clips, al-Zaytouna, Palestine Monitor, Social Sciences Magazines...] + art band + photographers + producers + programs anchors +journalists + in addition to other media and art experiences*"*.

Another example:

We have a seed for a *"comprehensive Dawa' educational"* organization: We have the Daw'a section in ISNA + Dr. Jamal Badawi Foundation + the center run by brother Harned al-Ghazali + the Dawa' center the Dawa' Committee and brother Shaker al-Sayyed are seeking to establish now + in addition to other Daw'a efforts here and there...*"*.

And this applies to all the organizations we call on establish- ing.

- The big challenge that is ahead of us is how to turn these seeds or *"scattered"* elements into comprehensive, stable, *"settled"* organizations that are connected with our Movement and which fly in our orbit and take orders from ow guidance. This does not prevent - but calls for - each central organization to have its local branches but its connection with the Islamic center in the city is a must.

- What is needed is to seek to prepare the atmosphere and the means to achieve *"the merger"* so that the sections, the committees, the regions, the branches and the Usras are eventually the heart and the core of these organizations.

Or, for the shift and the change to occur as follows:

1 - The Movement Department + The Secretariat Department
2- Education Department + Dawa'a Com. 3- Sisters Department
4- The Financial Department + Investment Committee + The Endowment
5- Youth Department + Youths Organizations Department
6- The Social Committee + Matrimony Committee + Mercy Foundation
7- The Security Committee
8- The Political Depart. + Palestine Com. 9- The Group's Court + The Legal
Com. 10- Domestic Work Department
1 1 - Our magazines + the print + our art band
12- The Studies Association + The Publication House + Dar al-Kitab
13- Scientific and Medical societies
14- The Organizational Conference
15- The Shura Council + Planning Com. 16- The Executive Office
17- The General Masul
18- The regions, branches & Usras
    - The Organizational & Administrative Organization - The General Center
    - Dawa' and Educational Organization - The Women's Organization
    - The Economic Organization
    - Youth Organizations
    - The Social Organization
    - The Security Organization
    - The Political Organization
    - The Judicial Organization
Its work is to be distributed to the rest of the organizations
    - The Media and Art Organization
    - The Intellectual & Cultural Organization
    - Scientific, Educational & Professional Organization
    - The Islamic-American Founding Conference
    - The Shura Council for the Islamic-American Movement
    - The Executive Office of the Islamic-American Movement
    - Chairman of the Islamic Movement and its official Spokesman
    - Field leaders of organizations & Islamic centers

Five: Comprehensive Settlement Organization:

- We would then seek and struggle in order to make each one of these above-mentioned organizations a *"comprehensive organization"* throughout the days and the years, and as long as we are destined to be in this country. What is important is that we put the foundation and we will be followed by peoples and generations that would finish the march and the road but with a clearly-defined guidance.

And, in order for us to clarify what we mean with the comprehensive, specialized organization, we mention here the characteristics and traits of each organization of the *"promising"* organizations.

1. From the Dawa' and educational aspect [The Dawa' and Educational Organization]: to include:
- The Organization to spread the Dawa' (Central and local branches).
- An institute to graduate Callers and Educators.
- Scholars, Callers, Educators, Preachers and Program Anchors,
- Art and communication technology, Conveyance and Dawa'.
- A television station.
- A specialized Dawa' magazine.
- A radio station.
- The Higher Islamic Council for Callers and Educators.
- The Higher Council for Mosques and Islamic Centers.
- Friendship Societies with the other religions... and things like that.

2. - Politically [The Political Organization]: to include:
- A central political party.
- Local political offices.
- Political symbols.
- Relationships and alliances.
- The American Organization for Islamic Political Action - Advanced Information Centers ... and things like that.

3. - Media [The Media and Art Organization]: to include:
- A daily newspaper.
- Weekly, monthly and seasonal magazines. - Radio stations.
- Television programs.
- Audio and visual centers.
- A magazine for the Muslim child.
- A magazine for the Muslim woman.
- A print and typesetting machines.
- A production office.
- A photography and recording studio
- Art bands for acting, chanting and theater.
- A marketing and art production office... and things like that.

4. - Economically [The Economic Organization]: to include: - An Islamic Central bank.

- Islamic endowments.
- Investment projects.
- An organization for interest-free loans... and things like that.

5. - Scientifically and Professionally [The Scientific, Educational and Professional Organization]: to include:

- Scientific research centers.
- Technical organizations and vocational training.
- An Islamic university.
- Islamic schools.
- A council for education and scientific research.
- Centers to train teachers.
- Scientific societies in schools.
- An office for academic guidance.
- A body for authorship and Islamic curricula....and things like that.

6. - Culturally and Intellectually [The Cultural and Intellectual Organization]: to include:

- A center for studies and research.
- Cultural and intellectual foundations such as [The Social Scientists Society
- Scientists and Engineers Society]
- An organization for Islamic thought and culture.
- A publication, translation and distribution house for Islamic books.
- An office for archiving, history and authentication
- The project to translate the Noble Quran, the Noble Sayings... and things like that.

7. - Socially [The Social-Charitable Organization]: to include:

- Social clubs for the youths and the community's sons and daughters
- Local societies for social welfare and the services are tied to the Islamic centers
- The Islamic Organization to Combat the Social Ills of the U .S. Society
- Islamic houses project
- Matrimony and family cases office... and things like that.

8. - Youths [The Youth Organization]: to include: - Central and local youths foundations.

- Sports teams and clubs

- Scouting teams... and things like that.

9.   - Women [The Women Organization]: to include:

- Central and local women societies.

- Organizations of training, vocational and housekeeping.

- An organization to train female preachers.

- Islamic kindergartens... and things like that.

10   - Organizationally and Administratively [The Administrative and Organizational Organization]: to include:

- An institute for training, growth, development and planning
- Prominent experts in this field
- Work systems, bylaws and Covenents fit for running the most complicated bodies and organizations
- A periodic magazine in Islamic development and administration.
- Owning camps and halls for the various activities. - A data, polling and census bank.
- An advanced communication network.
- An advanced archive for our heritage and production... and things like that.

11   - Security [The Security Organization]: to include:

- Clubs for training and learning self-defense techniques.
- A center which is concerned with the security issues [Technical, intellectual, technological and human]....and things like that.

12   - Legally [The Legal Organization]: to include:

- A Central Jurisprudence Council
- A Central Islamic Court.
- Muslim Attorneys Society.
- The Islamic Foundation for Defense of Muslims' Rights... and things like that.

And success is by God.

Attachment number (1)

A list of our organizations and the organizations of our friends

[Imagine if they all march according to one plan!!!]

1.	ISNA	= ISLAMIC SOCIETY OF NORTH AMERICA
2.	MSA	= MUSLIM STUDENTS' ASSOCIATION
3.	MCA	= THE MUSLIM COMMUNITIES ASSOCIATION
4.	AMSS	= THE ASSOCIATION OF MUSLIM SOCIAL SCIENTISTS
5.	AMSE	= THE ASSOCIATION OF MUSLIM SCIENTISTS AND ENGINEERS
6.	IMA	= ISLAMIC MEDICAL ASSOCIATION
7.	ITC	= ISLAMIC TEACHING CENTER
8.	NAIT	= NORTH AMERICAN ISLAMIC TRUSTS
9.	FID	= FOUNDATION FOR INTERNATIONAL DEVELOPMENT
10.	IHC	= ISLAMIC HOUSING COOPERATIVE
11.	ICD	= ISLAMIC CENTERS DIVISION
12.	ATP	= AMERICAN TRUST PUBLICATIONS
13.	AVC	= AUDIO-VISUAL CENTER
14.	IBS	= ISLAMIC BOOK SERVICE
15.	MBA	= MUSLIM BUSINESSMEN ASSOCIA TION
16.	MYNA	= MUSLIM YOUTH OF NORTH AMERICA
17.	IFC	= ISNA FIQH COMMITTEE
18.	IPAC	= ISNA POLITICAL AWARENESS COMMITTEE
19.	IED	= ISLAMIC EDUCATION DEPARTMENT
20.	MAYA	= MUSLIM ARAB YOUTH ASSOCIA TION
21.	MISG	= MALASIAN [sic] ISLAMIC STUDY GROUP
22.	IAP	= ISLAMIC ASSOCIATION FOR PALESTINE
23.	UASR	= UNITED ASSOCIA TION FOR STUDIES AND RESEARCH
24.	OLF	= OCCUPIED LAND FUND
25.	MIA	= MERCY INTERNA TIONAL ASSOCIA TION
26.	ICNA	= ISLAMIC CIRCLEOF NORTH AMERICA
27.	BMI	= BAITUL MAL INC
28.	IIIT	= INTERNATIONAL INSTITUTE FOR ISLAMIC THOUGHT
29.	IIC	= ISLAMIC INFORMATION CENTER

APPENDIX IV

In the name of God, the Beneficent, the Merciful

Islamic Action for Palestine –
An internal memo - October - 1992

One: Introduction:

Islam entered Palestine as it entered other parts of the earth. Palestine was honored by it and it lived under its shadow a while in time. To it, the best of the creation, God's prophet, peace be upon him, was journeyed and in it, the best of the humans led God's prophets, peace be upon them, in a prayer and a submission to the God of heavens and earth. And from it, he was taken to celestial galaxy where the Capable God is. Palestine is the blessed land whose dust was trodden by the horses of the Muslim conquerors and which was blessed by the arrival of Caliph Omar to receive the keys of Jerusalem. Palestine is the land which was protected and preserved by Muslims in the Rashidian, the Ommiades and then the Abbasi Dynasties. Palestine is the one whose land leader hero Saladin cleansed from the defilement of the Crusaders and on whose land the triumphant leader Qotoz conquered the invaders.

Palestine is a land which God the Almighty has honored with the blood of the Companions which watered its soil, Covenenting a path on which all great heroes such as al-Qassam, al-Husseini, al-Zeer, Jamjoum and al-Sa'adi and other Muslim grand men marched. Palestine is the land which moved from one honor to another by the arrival of representatives of the 20th century innovator, martyr Imam Hassan al-Banna, and they transferred to it the Muslim Brotherhood Movement and branches for the Ikhwan were formed in the cities of Palestine in the early 40's. Palestine is the one for which Muslim Brotherhood prepared armies - made up from the children of Islam in the Arab and Islamic nations - to liberate its land from the abomination and the defilement of the children of the Jews and they watered its pure soil with their honorable blood which sprouted into a Jihad that is continuing until the Day of Resurrection and provided a zeal without relenting making the slogan of its children "It is a Jihad for victory or martyrdom."

The Muslim Brotherhood Movement has cared for all the issues of Muslims considering that they are all one nation. And he who did not care about the issues of Muslims is not one of them as the chosen one said, God's prayers are upon him.

Yet, we noticed the concern of the Movement for the cause of Palestine fi-omits early beginnings and it enjoyed a special care from Guide Hassan al-

Banna, may God rest his soul. This special care is founded upon two main characteristics which the Palestinian cause enjoy separate from other Muslims' issues:

The 1st characteristic: is the fact that Palestine is a cause with a special Islamic status as it has Al-Aqsa mosque, third among the mosques which are to be visited. And it has the honorable Rock. It is the land of the Night Journey and the Ascension. It is the land of the great crowd and it is a holy and a blessed land according to the text of Noble Quran. Its land was watered with the blood of the martyrs from the Companions, the Followers and others along the ages. It has also graduated genius scholars such as al-Shafei, al-Nabolosi, al-Ajlouni and others.

The 2nd characteristic: comes from the fact that the struggle is with the Jews who do not constitute a danger to Palestine alone, but a danger to Arabs and Muslims in their homelands, resources, religion, traditions, influence and political entity. Due to the Jewish influence in different global nations specially America and Europe, the struggle in Palestine has a degree of entanglement and complexity, or junctions and contradictions between international politics like no other cause in the world. Due to this entanglement and complexity, no Arab or Muslim nation or a nation with an impact on international politics has not been affected by this struggle either negatively or positively.

These two characteristics make the cause of Palestine a unique cause which requires a unique method and means to manage the struggle as well. This is what the Islamic Movement - the Muslim Brotherhood - has realized. Therefore, it paid a special attention to the cause of Palestine and established a special apparatus for it which requires support and assistance from all the Brotherhood's movements.

Two: The Foundation of Islamic Action for Palestine:

The "worry for Palestine" and the liberation of the homeland and the worshipers in it has not been a passing worry in the soul, mind and programs of the Islamic Movement, but it has been a true and a sincere worry even if it took on several shapes and went through different stages.

Years after their march of building and educating the desired Muslim generation, and after about four decades, The Muslim Brotherhood in Palestine have realized that there is no escape the unity merger between the two branches of the Muslim Brotherhood in Jordan and Palestine and this was in the beginning of 1978 after the leadership of the Movement then realized that action for Palestine requires the unity of the Muslim nation and that this unity must be preceded by the unity of Islamic action. Thus, came the first initiative which was the foundation of the Muslim Brotherhood in the Sharnm Countries. The Brotherhood action for Palestine through the Shamm countries went through several stages with positives and negatives in every stage.

A- The Palestine Section:

At the end of the seventies, the Shamm Countries Movement opened a new section which was called "The Palestine Section" to oversee the affairs of the Ikhwan inside the Occupied Territories. It was considered the liaison between the followers of the Movement inside and outside.

In the beginning of the eighties, the Islamic action for Palestine experienced distinguished leaps. At the inside level, groups and apparatuses were formed to confront the Zionist enemy and they carried different names then such as "The Palestinian Mujahedeen" and other names. At the outside level, a number of associations, Islamic youths and students unions were formed to ally the masses in order to render the Palestinian cause victorious. Therefore, the Islamic Association for Palestine's Students in Kuwait, the Islamic Association for Palestinian Youths in Britain, the Islamic Association for Palestine in North America and Muslim Palestinian Youths Association in Germany and others were founded.

B- Palestine Conference:

In October 1983, the first conference for Palestine at the Sharnm countries level was organized. Based on the recommendations of this conference and the feelings of the Ikhwan in the executive office of the importance of paying a special attention to Palestinian action, a decision was made to broaden the powers of the Palestine Section and to reorganize it to be called "The General Apparatus for Palestine" in the fall of 1985.

C- The Central Committee for Associations and Palestinian Students Unions:

In the same year, 1983, the Movement established an organizational frame which encompasses all these Palestinian associations and unions and coordinates between them to serve the same cause. A Shura Council was formed for this frame and an executive committee to oversee its financial, administrative and planning affairs. This was done following an agreement and a blessing from the Muslim Brotherhood in the Shamm Countries and the Guidance Office of the International Movement.

D- Palestine Committees in the countries:

With the growth of the blessed Intifada and the spread of the spirit of Jihad amidst the children of Palestine and the nation, it became incumbent upon the remainder of the Ikhwan branches to play a role in attributing this Intifada and this Islamic action to Palestine. Therefore, a resolution was issued by the Guidance Office and the Shura Council of the International Movement to form "Palestine Committees" in all the Arab, the Islamic and the Western nations whose job is to make the Palestinian cause victorious and to support it with what it needs of media, money, men and all of that. (Refer to the resolution in the supplement).

Three: a- The Islamic Resistance Movement:

With the increase of the Intifada and the advance of the Islamic action inside and outside Palestine, the Islamic Resistance Movement (Hamas), provided through its activities in resisting the Zionist occupation a lot of sacrifices from martyrs, detainees, wounded, injured, fugitives and deportees and it was able to prove that it is an original and an effective movement in leading the Palestinian people. This Movement - which was bred in the bosom of the mother movement, "The Muslim Brotherhood" - restored hope and life to the Muslim nation and the notion that the flare of Jihad has not died out and that the banner of Islamic Jihad is still raised.

But, the law of God the Almighty which does not change or alter willed that the Movement go through harsh consecutive trials which started in 1989 as the leadership of the Movement was arrested and held in prison where it still is, followed by the second and the third leaderships in consecutive months. But, God the Almighty has made available to the blessed Movement generations of leaders who were prepared for such days and such circumstances. Due to the successive strikes and continuous arrests in the ranks of the leaders in particular, the General Apparatus for Palestine became the acting central leadership for the Islamic Resistance Movement (Hamas) in the inside and the outside.

b-The Organization

Structure of the Movement:

The organizational structure consists of two organizations which are:

1- The Consulting Council: It includes **50** members from the inside and the outside, representatives of the International Office of Guidance and Shura and representatives of the executive office and the Shura Council for the Shamm countries in addition to a number of distinguished Brotherhood personalities in the Arab and Muslim nations.

2- The Executive Committee: It includes **11** members who lead the Islamic action for Palestine in the inside and the outside. Many technical and specialized committees in the fields of politics, media, finance are led by them as well as a number of organizations and centers which serve the goals of the general apparatus and the resistance movement in the inside and the outside.

And the Movement (Hamas) is represented in several of the leadership councils which are affiliated with the Guidance Office. They are:

1. The Shura Office of the International Movement.
2. The Guidance Office.
3. The Guidance Office for the Shamm countries.
4. The Executive Office for the Sharnm countries.

The Movement submits to these entities reports, studies, plans, bylaws and work projects for approval and signature or modifications and guidance. Several resolutions relating to the cause and the Movement have been made which we will mention in the next items, God's willing.

C- The relationship of the Movement and its offices:

With the broadening of the Movement, the increase of the resistance and the political weight the Movement began to experience due to its stands, statements, relationships and projects, it opened several political offices in some of the Arab and Islamic countries. The

Movement has reached a number of dual and collective agreements through its continuous meetings with the Palestinian factions, the Islamic and the nationalistic among them. It still hopes to continue to increase the scope of its relationship with all Arab, Islamic and international sides and fields.

Four: Some of the resolutions reached by the Guidance Office regard in the Palestinian Cause:

To affirm the status of the cause on the agenda of the Ikhwan in the General Guidance Office, they have reached a number of resolutions, most important of which are:

Supporting the continuation of the Intifada. The Ikhwan in the countries are to hold fundraising campaigns to support the Intifada.

The Guidance Office is to adopt a policy which affirms that the Palestinian cause is the grand central cause to all the Muslim Ikhwan in the world.

Notifying the countries that the Palestine Section which is affiliate with the Shamrn countries is the one in charge of action for the Palestinian cause. No other entity is to be listened to regarding this cause.

The cause of Palestine is the cause of the Movement and is given the proper attention through its organizations considering that the Palestine Section is a part of the Sharnm countries movement.

Stressing to the countries the need to form special committees for Palestine in each country.

Notifying the countries to provide the following according to the vision of the general apparatus for Palestine, according to their ability and in coordination with the apparatus while documenting it with the countries:

a- Media support b- Political support c- Financial support.

Organizational support to facilitate communication with the Ikhwan of the Shamrn countries in their organizations and to pass the programs for internal mobilization to the remainder of the Ikhwan.

Benefitting from the Ikhwan's relationships in all fields with the various factions in the countries. The completion of formation of Palestine committees in all the countries and giving attention to holding conferences relating to Palestine while publicizing and focusing on the savagery of the Jews.

Asking the countries to contact the international organizations and boards to denounce the crimes of the Jews in Palestine.

Forming an international Islamic front for the cause of Palestine. Developing the work of Palestine committees in all the countries and forming committees for Palestine in the countries where they are not formed yet.

Calling upon all the Ikhwan to increase financial support from them and from others so that the brothers in charge of the Palestine action can fulfill the work requirements.

15. Holding conferences to make Al-Aqsa and Palestine victorious and to fight surrendering solutions.
16. Reviving the Palestinian cause with the public opinion by issuing edicts and giving speeches and lectures.
17. **Asking the countries to increase the financial and the moral support for Hamas.**

Five: Islamic Action for the Palestinian Cause in North America:

Like other Western, Arab and Islamic arenas, the American arena has seen a move for action for the Palestinian cause by the grace of God and due to the presence of the Islamic Movement and its pioneer the Muslim Brotherhood Movement. The first organizational frame for Islamic action for Palestine came in the beginning of the eighties when the leadership of the Movement decided to establish "The Islamic Association for Palestine in North America." The Association was and still is the general field through which the Movement expresses its view and positions regarding the Palestinian cause. When work developed, the Intifada started and the Islamic Resistance Movement (Hamas) was formed and the general apparatus for Palestine developed, and in light of the resolutions of the Guidance Office and the Shura Council of the International Movement to form Palestine committees in all the countries, the General Director of the apparatus came and met with the leadership of the Movement in America in 1988. After discussions and agreement, a "Palestine Committee" was formed under the supervision of the executive office. The Committee was then tasked with supervising all the organizations which serve the plan of the Movement domestically and internationally in addition to the Palestinian cause. Among these organizations were "The Islamic Association," "the Occupied Land Fund" and "The United Association." Like other directors of the Movement's committees and sections, the director of Palestine Committee is to submit periodical reports and adheres to the directions and the guidance of the leadership of the Group.

The president of the Islamic Association for Palestine is considered a member in the youths organizations section which is affiliated with the executive office and is treated like other organizations (such as the Association, the Students' Society and the Malaysian Students' Society...). The Association presents its plan and budget (which includes opening new branches for The

Association, holding festivals, conferences and such things) like other organizations to the section to approve it and then implement it.

Six: The essence and the needed role:

After the previous presentation about the historical status of Palestine and the importance of liberating the blessed land, the land of the Night Journey and the Ascension, the first prayer niche and the third holiest site, after the presentation about the developments of Islamic action for this cause, the role of the Islamic Movement and - and on top of it, the Muslim Brotherhood - with all pride and cherish, and after mentioning some of the resolutions reached by the highest organizational authority within the Muslim Brotherhood Movement represented by the Shura Council and the Guidance Office of the International Movement, after all these presentations, a reader might pose a question: Why this memo? And why now?

*** As for why this memo?**
It is in order to tell our brothers and our beloved, the children of this blessed call, that their cause, Palestine, has not been forgotten and that it is always the number one item on the meeting agenda of the Guidance Office and the International Shura Council, and in order to tell our Palestinian brothers in particular that we are with them as their cause and the duty to serve it is not for them alone, but that we compete with them in it hoping for the reward and the recompense, and hoping to receive martyrdom on the soil of the holy land and in the shadows of Al-Aqsa mosque.

Also, to tell our brothers and beloved ones, the children of this great call from the different nationalities, that our dealing with the Palestinian cause is not from a national or regional prospective - far be it from us - but it is mandated by Islam and the creed in order to move, exert effort and are not meager.

*** As for why now?**
It is order to confirm to all, Palestinians and other nationalities (which we never believed in or recognized them as they are just mere geographical divisions and nothing more) that unity and cohesion of one Islamic-Ikhwani wall in face of the conspiracy to sell Palestine and to hand over Jerusalem to God's enemy and our enemy, all of which in exchange for a submissive, fragile administrative self-rule, is needed today more than any past day.

The Palestinian cause – or say the Islam's cause in Palestine – needs today an effective and a distinguished role for the grand Islamic Movement as one fortified wall behind its leadership represented by the Shura Council and a strong support for their tool and striking wing, the Islamic Resistance Movement (Hamas).

To conclude this memo, we stress to our brothers the need to stand behind this blessed Islamic action so that God the Almighty make it, or make available to us through it, a field for Jihad in which we teach the enemies of God the lessons of prophets and Mujahedeen in triumphing over them or martyring for the sake of God. And God is provider of success.

ABOUT THE AUTHOR

Ilana Freedman is a veteran intelligence analyst specializing in Islamic terrorism. Trained in Israel, where she lived for sixteen years, she has been tracking and analyzing Islamic terrorism for over three decades. She has authored several hundred articles published in the national and international press and on her blogs at GerardDirect.com and FreedmanReport.com.

Freedman is also the author of *JIHAD! Understanding the Threat of the Islamic State in America;* and *Gateway to Jihad: Tablighi Jama'at,* Volumes I and II of the "Terror Jihad Readers Series," published by The Center for Security Policy.

INDEX

www.ingramcontent.com/pod-product-compliance
Lightning Source LLC
Chambersburg PA
CBHW050913260726
48660CB00001B/175